*Special thanks
to Kevin Musgrave for his careful proof-reading
and many insightful suggestions,
to Jeff Musgrave for his inspired cover design,
and to our mothers for their encouragement.*

Cover design by Jeff Musgrave — www.jeffmusgrave.com

INDISPENSABLE MARKETING STRATEGIES

*How to Outwit Your Competition,
Attract and Retain Customers,
and Multiply Your Profits*

Powerful Marketing Strategy Secrets
for Profitable Small Business Management

Paul Francis Musgrave, MBA

Illustrated by Machiko Yamane Musgrave

Published by April Avenue Media

Indispensable Marketing Strategies, 2nd Edition
Copyright © 2008 by Paul Francis Musgrave.
All rights reserved. No part of this book may be reproduced in any manner whatsoever, or stored in a retrieval system, or transmitted in any form or by any means, electronic, mechanical, photocopying, recording, scanning, or otherwise without written permission, except in the case of brief quotations embodied in critical articles or reviews.

Published by April Avenue Media, Canada.
For more information, visit www.IndispensableStrategies.com

Any brand names, trademarks, and service marks that appear in this book are mentioned for purposes of illustration, criticism, and analysis only.

The author, publisher, distributors, and retailers of this book make no representations or warranties regarding its usefulness, and assume no liability for any claims, losses, or damages. Your use of this book is entirely at your own risk. This publication is intended to provide accurate and authoritative information in regard to the subject matter covered. It is sold on the understanding that the author and publisher are not engaged in providing legal, accounting, or other professional services. If such assistance is required, you are advised to obtain the help of a competent professional.

Musgrave, Paul Francis.
   Indispensable Marketing Strategies: How to Outwit Your Competition, Attract and Retain Customers, and Multiply Your Profits - Marketing Strategy Secrets for Profitable Small Business Management /
   Paul Francis Musgrave
   Includes bibliographical references and index.
   ISBN 978-0-9781277-6-3

Library of Congress Subject Headings:
1. Strategic Planning   2. Business Strategy   3. Marketing Planning & Strategy   4. Small Business   5. Branding (Marketing)   6. Marketing Channels   7. Advertising – Brand Name Products   8. Marketing Management   9. New Products – Marketing   10. Startup Companies   11. Brand Name Products   12. Business Planning   13. Competition   14. Customer Relations   15. Entrepreneurship

BUS043000   Business & Economics / Marketing / General
BUS041000   Business & Economics / Management
BUS063000   Business & Economics / Strategic Planning
BUS060000   Business & Economics / Small Business
BUS002000   Business & Economics / Advertising & Promotion
BUS025000   Business & Economics / Entrepreneurship

2.01.02

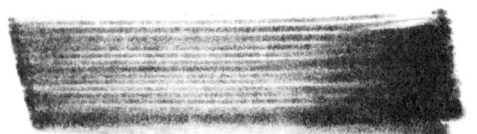

Contents

A Strategic Marketing Short Story 1

Envision a Bright Future for Your Firm 29

The Secrets of Successful Segmentation 45

Position Your Product for Customer Trust 71

Leverage Your Brand Equity 109

Be in the Right Place at the Right Time 129

What is Your Profit Potential? 137

Secure a Strategic Advantage 159

Pricing Strategies Simplified 173

Treacherous Distribution Channel Dynamics 181

What Are Your Strategic Priorities? 209

Strategies for Gaining and Retaining Market Share 215

Notes 231

Bibliography 232

Index 233

Chapter 1

A Strategic Marketing Short Story

Success. What does it mean to you? In business, one way to measure success is by sales and profits. Offer something that people want, and you will generate sales. Control your costs, and you might earn some profits. Sounds simple? In reality, business success is typically far more complicated. But let's not delve into the complexities yet. To introduce the concepts of strategic marketing most effectively, let's start with a simplified version of reality. Tongue-in-cheek, we'll imagine living in a world without mass production, the Internet, or **antitrust laws**. Let's watch as people in our imaginary world discover and use the basic principles of marketing strategy, in pursuit of business success.

Our imaginary world revolves around one of several small communities located in an isolated mountain valley. In our community, named Latherville, many local residents are farmers, while others manufacture goods at home. These local manufacturers typically specialize in a narrow range of products that they alone supply. For example, Wendy Wellington weaves woolen cloth at home, and sells it from a stall at the local craft market. By specializing, Wendy has become an expert at weaving woolens, and she weaves high quality cloth with great skill. Because

> **Antitrust laws** forbid certain business practices that reduce competition. These laws can vary widely across regions. Be sure to find out about any competition laws affecting the conduct of business in your area, so that you'll know if any particular marketing strategies or tactics are prohibited.

she weaves so much, she has become very organized and efficient. This allows her to sell her woolens at attractive prices. Like Wendy, the other local manufacturers have each become experts at making their particular products. To take advantage of each other's skill and efficiency, they buy each other's products in the local market.

One particular local resident, Sally Smith, enjoys tinkering with basic chemistry. She has set up a lab in her barn, and after some months of experimentation, has invented a brand-new substance that she calls "soap". After receiving positive feedback from friends and neighbors who have tried her soap, Sally works up her courage, and borrows enough money to establish a soap business. She starts manufacturing her soap in her barn, and opens a shop in town where she can sell it. By handing out samples with instructions to passersby in the street, she introduces her new product to the community. Word quickly spreads that her wonderful new substance can help people wash themselves, their clothes, and all sorts of things. Customers flock to her store to purchase soap for their cleansing needs, and Sally's soap is suddenly a success.

The Soap Product Life Cycle

The development and introduction of Sally's soap has marked the start of a new product life cycle. A **product**

life cycle (PLC) describes the demand for a product category over time. Product life cycles typically start with a development stage, which is a period of secret experimentation, known as research and development, or R&D. This corresponds with the many months Sally spends in her barn, experimenting with various chemicals, until she perfects her soap formula. During this period, she risks her time and money, without any assurance that she will ever generate sales and profits from her product.

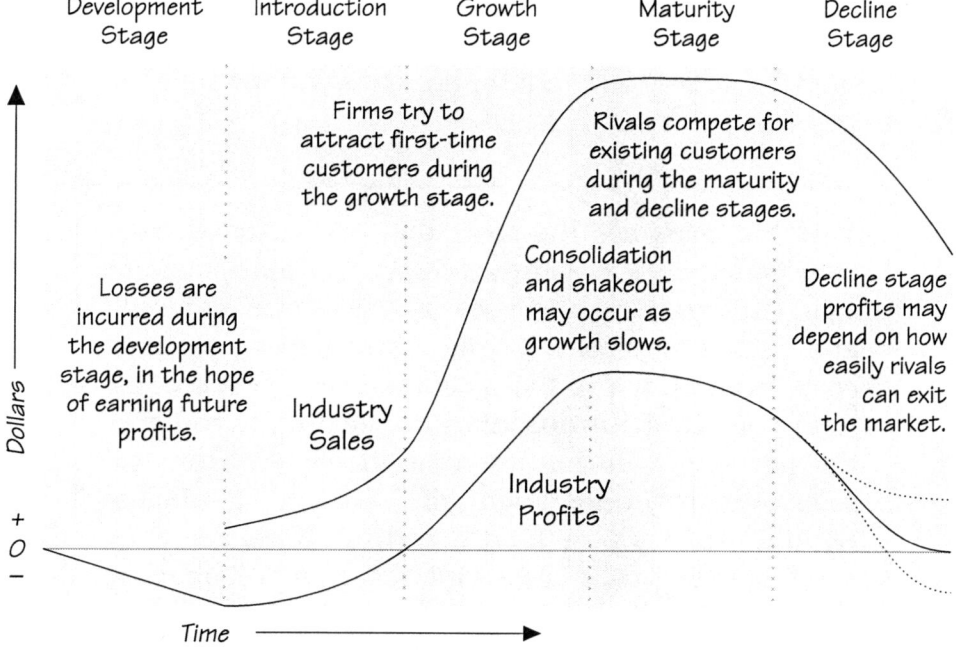

Stages of the Product Life Cycle

To **incur** means to be subjected to the effect of something negative, such as a cost.

In the introduction stage that follows, Sally gives hundreds of free soap samples to potential customers, hoping to make them aware of her product. Though each soap bar she sells generates a small profit, these profits are initially consumed by the cost of the free samples she hands out.

How does Sally know that her business is not yet profitable? Sally explains the math to her husband like this: "Each bar of soap that I sell for a dollar costs me 60 cents to make and sell. That leaves me a **contribution margin** of 40 cents on each bar sold. I sold 100 bars of soap this month. And so, 40 cents contribution margin per bar x 100 bars = $40 **total contribution margin**. However, I also gave away samples that cost me $50 to make, which is $10 more than my total contribution margin. So I am $10 poorer than I was last month, not counting the rent I had to pay for my store."

> **Variable costs** are the costs that are incurred each time you sell one of your products. Examples include sales commissions, and your product's raw materials and packaging costs. If you subtract these variable costs from your product's selling price, you are left with your **contribution margin** per unit. If you add the per unit contribution margin earned from all sales of your product, you will have your **total contribution margin**, or **total margin dollars**. For your product to be profitable, its total margin dollars must exceed its fixed marketing costs, such as advertising, marketing research, and free samples.

Upon hearing this, her husband urges her to close the business immediately, before losing even more money. Sally replies that she too would prefer to avoid taking any financial risks. But she insists that initially, all businesses must spend money to get started, and that patience is necessary while waiting for profits to follow at a later time. That time will come, she hopes, during the **growth stage** of the PLC, when her soap will be increasing in popularity, and will attract purchases even from the residents of neighboring communities.

She expects that later on, in the **maturity stage** of the PLC, everyone in the valley will know about her soap. There might be no new customers to attract, but her

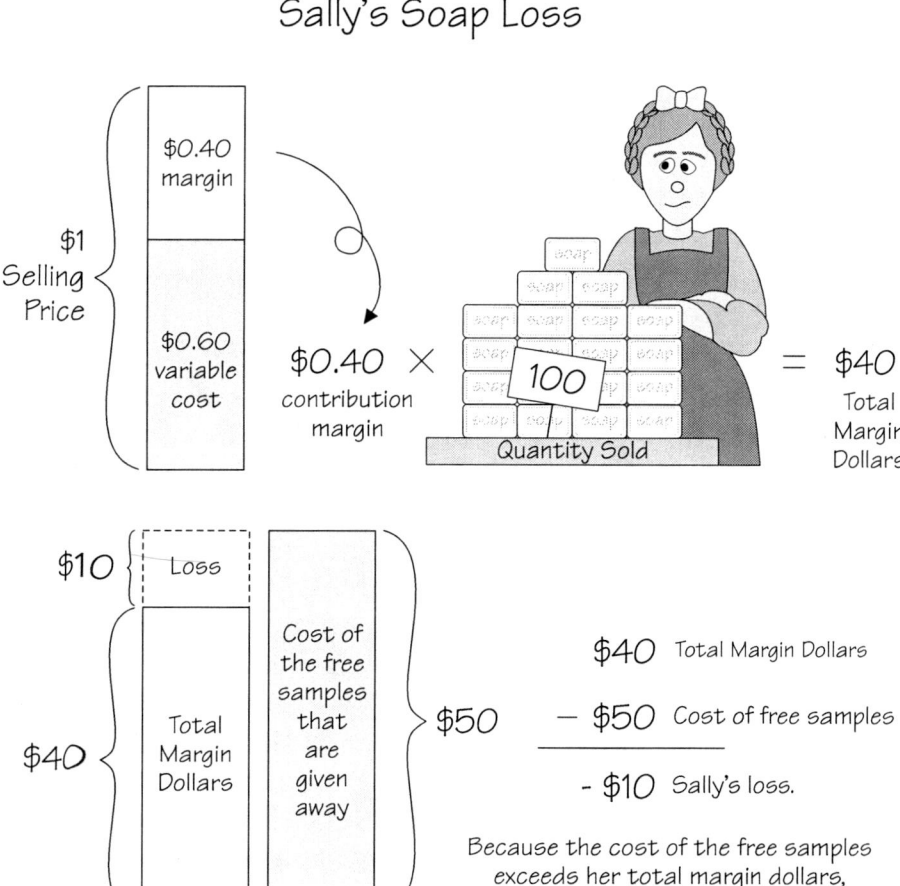

business will hopefully earn steady profits from the repeat purchases of her numerous existing customers. Of course, some customers will grow old and die, but they will be replaced by new, younger customers. Thus, she believes that in the maturity stage, her business will remain stable and profitable.

Sally is also comforted by the thought that people will always want to use soap. She believes she will never need to experience the **decline stage** of the soap PLC, during which demand would decrease, profits could collapse, and soap manufacturers might fight each other desperately for the remaining customers. She believes the soap industry will probably never reach this stage, unless people decide not to wash anymore.

Sally has high hopes for her business, but even as she talks to her husband, plots are hatching that will change the course of events in ways that she has not anticipated. Her business success has attracted the attention of other aspiring entrepreneurs, such as Larry Lightfoot.

Success Attracts Imitation

Excited by the success of Sally's sensational soap, Larry sets up a soap lab in his own barn. In an attempt to duplicate Sally's success, he creates a soap of his own that is very similar to Sally's. After selling his soap in his store, Larry starts to realize that Sally has an advantage: When people think of soap, they think of Sally. Her soap has **top-of-the-mind awareness** among consumers. Her reputation is growing fast, while Larry's soap remains relatively unknown. Though Larry is encouraged that his sales are growing at 10% a year, he is shocked when he learns that Sally's sales are growing at an astounding 50% annually. Her business is getting bigger faster, and Larry is falling farther and farther behind. In addition, Larry is only one of many new manufacturers who have entered the soap market. The industry has become crowded and competitive.

> When customers experience a need, they will initially consider the products that they think of first, which are those that enjoy **top-of-the-mind awareness**.

Larry ponders his predicament. He knows that his success will depend on consumers' purchase decisions. "Their decisions are motivated by their needs," he thinks to himself. "If I can discover washing needs that are not being satisfied, then perhaps I will be able to create new soaps that can satisfy those needs. Then I will not have to compete directly with Sally."

By conversing with customers, Larry learns of their unsatisfied needs. Most cannot quite say exactly what they would like, and they cannot imagine all of the things that soap could be. Larry encourages them patiently with questions like, "If you could have a special soap that would be perfect for your laundry, what would it be like?" Larry listens, and tries to imagine even needs that his customers have difficulty describing. He makes a list of soap ideas, and works in his barn each evening, hoping to create new soaps that will satisfy his customers. But even one new soap formula can take many months to develop. And time is running out, as competition in the soap market is frothing up.

The Shakeout

By now, most people in the valley have learned about soap. Since new customers are becoming hard to find, sales growth has almost stopped. The growth stage of the soap PLC is coming to an end, and the maturity stage is beginning.

The soap manufacturers sorely miss the excitement of rapid growth, and they become frustrated and restless. For new sources of growth, they start targeting each other's customers with advertising and promotions. This eventually provokes a price war, triggered by a single manufacturer, who cuts his prices in the hope of stealing some market share. Determined to keep their customers, his rivals refuse to be undersold, and they match every discount.

Before long, soap is selling at a 40% discount. Like all the other small firms, Larry is selling his soap at $0.60 a bar. This covers only his variable costs, leaving no contribution margin to cover his fixed costs. As a result, Larry is living on his savings, hoping for better days.

Meanwhile, with all the low-priced soap available, consumers have stocked up. This will enable them to resist any price increases, until they have used up all the cheap soap they have stored in their cupboards. Times are indeed tough in the soap business. And worse is yet to come.

> When a manufacturer temporarily reduces the price of a product, retailers and consumers may purchase more than they presently need, to avoid having to purchase it later at the regular price. This purchasing behavior is known as **forward buying**.

With the onset of the price war, Sally has been reluctant to match her rivals' price cuts, as that would entail sacrificing her margins. "I still have almost 80% of the market, and I have lost very little market share," she thinks to herself. "Even if I increase my share to 90%, the price cuts necessary to achieve that could decrease my total margin dollars. So I think I'll just keep my prices where they are." But as her market share losses continue, she starts to consider price cuts – just to keep her remaining customers.

Lamenting the disorderly soap industry, Sally wonders, "Why can't my rivals see that they are just hurting themselves with their price cuts? Lowering their prices only invites retaliation. They all have the same costs, and so none of them can gain any advantage."

> Large firms tend to purchase their production materials and other supplies in large quantities. This gives them negotiating leverage when purchasing, so they can obtain these items at a lower cost. For the same reason, they may be able to finance their business at lower rates, and advertise more economically. As well, their size allows them to hire more specialized employees, resulting in greater efficiency. Enabling them to operate at a lower cost, these advantages are known as **economies of scale**. Companies can also learn how to operate more efficiently and effectively by virtue of their accumulated experience. These advantages are known as **experience curve effects**.

Gradually, discouragement and bankruptcy thin the soap producers' ranks, leaving only the strongest to fight on. But if Sally enters the fray, she could defeat them all, because she has the lowest per-unit variable costs. That is, with by far the highest production volume, she enjoys the greatest **economies of scale**. For this reason, she is able to produce each bar of soap more cheaply than her rivals can. Moreover, having accumulated a great deal of soap production experience, she has learned to be more efficient than her rivals. Thus, she enjoys what are known as **experience curve effects.**

"Because of my lower costs, I earn more profit on every bar of soap that I sell. And I sell more bars of soap than all of my rivals combined," she explains to her husband. "My total margin dollars far exceed my marketing costs and my company overhead. My rivals are barely covering theirs."

Sally's cost advantages could enable her to beat her rivals' prices, if she chooses to. Why then, have her rivals started a price war that Sally could surely win? Are they counting on Sally's **mixed motives**, knowing that she will be loath to sacrifice her comfortable income with drastic price cuts?

> When you are faced with a decision, and each of your options have both advantages and disadvantages, you may experience **mixed motives** – or a state of indecisiveness. Sally is experiencing mixed motives because she wants to retain her market share, but must sacrifice her profit in order to do so.

Sally is indeed reluctant to react. "Do I really need to compete on price?" she asks. "I make much more soap than anyone. With all my experience, I have learned all the tricks of the trade, and I make a better bar of soap than any of my rivals. With such good quality, my customers won't leave me. Will they?" But leave her they do, gradually, and steadily, as the price war drags on from one week to the next. "I am losing my business! I must retaliate!" she exclaims to her husband one day. "If my customers do not appreciate the high quality of my soap, then I will

Sally's Rivals Don't Stand a Chance

Because of her higher sales volume, Sally can make each bar of soap at a much lower cost than any of her rivals. Thus, she can sell her soap at 10 cents below their cost, and still earn a 40% margin.

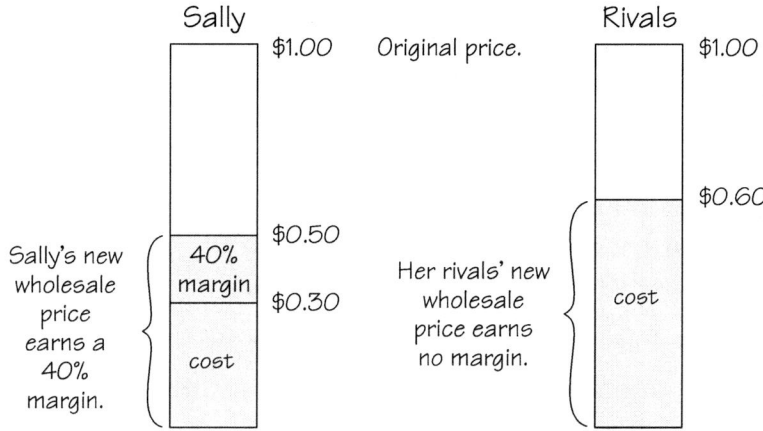

compete on price. I will teach my rivals a lesson they will not soon forget!"

Her husband tries to assure her that most of her customers do appreciate the quality of her soap. Perhaps it is just a few defectors who do not care about her quality. But as the defections continue, she realizes that her customers are not as satisfied as she has believed.

However, before addressing that issue, she resolves to end the price war, once and for all. She knows that with her experience and her economies of scale, her variable costs are just 30 cents per bar. "If I sell my soap at 50 cents per bar, I will still earn a 40% contribution margin," she thinks to herself. "My rivals' variable costs are 60 cents per bar. So if they match my 50 cent wholesale price, they will lose 10 cents per bar." And so she slashes her prices in half, to $0.50 a bar, ensuring that no rival can make a profit. One by one, realizing that they are beaten, Sally's rivals lose interest in the soap market, and turn their attention elsewhere.

The end of the growth stage of the soap product life cycle has brought an industry shakeout. In other words, intensified competition has caused the weaker firms to exit the market. The result is a much more consolidated industry structure, with Sally controlling a 98% share of the market, while Larry retains just 2%. This allows Sally to gradually raise her prices again, with Larry thankfully following her lead. With growth stalled and just one dominant firm remaining, the market has entered its maturity stage. But the maturity stage will not bring an end to the conflict. Sally's victory is only temporary.

> When market growth slows, first-time customers become rare. To continue growing, firms may start competing for each others' existing customers. Expensive promotions and price cuts can force the weakest firms out of business. Or they may be purchased by their larger rivals. This *shakeout* typically results in industry **consolidation**, whereby a handful of surviving firms emerge to dominate the market.

Frontal Attack Folly

Larry has learned a hard lesson. He thinks to himself, "I should never have attempted a frontal attack against an established competitor. My product features were similar to Sally's, so there was never any special reason for customers to switch to my soap. Besides, Sally's quality is better than mine. Once my rivals started cutting their prices, I had to cut mine too, to remain competitive. But Sally had the lowest costs, and that allowed her to retaliate with price cuts that no one could match. I lost this battle before it even started."

> The characteristics of your product, along with its price, the way you promote it, and the outlets where it is sold, are known as your **marketing mix**. These marketing mix elements are also known as **the four Ps**: product, price, promotion, and place of sale.

A **frontal attack** is an attempt to use a **marketing mix** that closely matches a rival's marketing mix, in order to steal their best-served customers. Larry launched a frontal attack against Sally by imitating her marketing mix. He failed for this reason, and because he attempted to compete against her considerable strengths. Specifically, her soap was higher in quality and enjoyed high consumer awareness. Moreover, her experience and economies of scale were superior. Instead of a frontal attack, Larry should have considered a **flanking attack**, to focus his efforts against Sally's weaknesses.

> A **flanking attack** involves attempting to gain market share by targeting customers that a rival serves poorly.

After some contemplation, Larry comes to this very conclusion himself. "People use Sally's soap for everything, but there are some uses for which it is not well suited. Sally's soap is mild enough for washing your face, but it is not strong enough for cleaning grease and grime from laundry. This is a weak point that Sally seems unaware of. Perhaps I could exploit it by selling a soap that is strong enough to clean laundry. I will not need to compete directly with Sally, because her soap is too mild for laundry grime."

In the ensuing months, Larry returns to his barn again for countless hours of secret experimentation with soap ingredients. At long last, the day comes when his liquid laundry soap is ready for market. He prepares hundreds of free samples, and hands them out around town – along with a leaflet explaining how his soap cleans laundry more effectively than Sally's soap does. People are fascinated with his liquid laundry soap, and are eager to try it with their next load of laundry. Upon doing so, they are immediately amazed at its effectiveness, and become Larry's loyal customers. Larry is delighted at successfully capturing a significant share of the soap market. "But is this mere luck?" Larry wonders. "Why have I succeeded on my second try?" he asks himself.

At this point, we need to pause the story for a moment so that we can analyze what has happened.

How Differentiation Differs from Positioning

Larry succeeded in his second attempt at entering the soap market by unknowingly employing two basic marketing techniques: Differentiation and positioning. **Differentiation** means making your product different from your rivals' products. **Positioning** means influencing consumers' *beliefs* about what makes your product special.

For example, Larry has differentiated his soap – ensuring that it differs from Sally's – by making it chemically stronger, so that it can cut through grease and grime. By solving laundry cleaning problems that Sally's soap does not properly address, Larry has launched a flanking attack.

Just as importantly, consumers *perceive* Larry's soap as being different from Sally's. Through his marketing communications, Larry has influenced consumers' beliefs, positioning his soap in their minds as the best product for cleaning laundry.

Positioning affects people's *beliefs* about a product, while differentiation affects the product *itself*. Differentiation and positioning normally work hand-in-hand. Generally, you should try to differentiate your product so that you can avoid a head-on confrontation with your rivals. As well, you should position your product distinctively, in a way that is compatible with its actual benefits. Larry has done this with his laundry liquid: His product is differentiated by virtue of its powerful grease-cutting formulation, and he has positioned it by emphasizing its laundry-cleaning benefits. His soap's positioning is consistent with its differentiation; consumers believe it is an effective laundry soap, and in fact it is. As a result, consumers now strongly associate his soap with effective laundry cleaning.

Larry's positioning has a further advantage: It is more focused than Sally's. Sally's broad all-purpose positioning was initially accepted by consumers. But that was early in the product life cycle, while they were still naïve about soap. Then, as they gained soap-use experience, they started to perceive the contradictions in Sally's positioning. In particular, they started to doubt that her soap could be both mild enough for their faces and tough enough for their laundry. They increasingly found Sally's broad positioning unrealistic, contradictory, and doubtful. This weakened their commitment and loyalty to her soap, leaving them more receptive to the attractively-priced competitors' soaps offered during the price war. Thus, Sally was forced to join the fray, and compete on price, along with her rivals.

Now that Larry's laundry liquid has arrived in the market, it seems to be the answer to a problem that Sally's soap has never properly addressed. Larry's soap promises to solve a single problem – tough laundry grime. This seems a realistic and credible claim. Larry's positioning builds trust by promising realistic benefits that his soap actually delivers. As a result, consumers believe and trust his soap, and this has propelled his laundry soap sales.

Larry's flanking attack has succeeded largely because he has astutely differentiated and positioned his soap to satisfy needs that Sally's soap does not. Though consumers still buy Sally's soap for most uses, they no longer use her soap to clean their laundry. She is disappointed to see her sales decline somewhat, but her business continues to thrive on sales of soap for general use. Now she wonders, "Should I launch a laundry liquid to compete with Larry's?" But before she can make up her mind, the soap business starts to become even more complicated.

Sam Singer Starts Selling Soap

Through the course of Sally's success, the business of soap has become an enduring obsession for an aspiring entrepreneur named Sam Singer. As a former soap manufacturer, defeated in the price war, Sam is still tormented by dreams of soap success. He has closely watched the launch of Larry Lightfoot's laundry liquid. Ever skeptical of Larry's prospects, Sam thinks to himself, "If Sally formulates her own laundry liquid, she may be able to manufacture it at a much lower cost than Larry can. She may decide to sell below his cost, putting him out of business before he has a chance to cause her more trouble."

Despite his misgivings, Sam has himself been hard at work for months now, formulating a whole line of personal soaps. He has developed a soap for every purpose, it seems. He has soaps for men, soaps for women, soaps for teenagers, soaps for children, soaps for babies, soaps for dry skin, and soaps for oily skin. Some soaps are scented, and others are not.

"Why so many soaps?" his wife asks.

"Because I have segmented the soap market," he replies. "I have divided the soap market into groups of consumers – or segments – according to their particular cleansing needs. I am going to sell a different kind of soap to each segment. By selling each segment a soap that is more suitable to their particular needs, I'll satisfy consumers better than Sally does."

The soap market can be divided into segments of customers who have different needs, attitudes, behaviors, and demographics.

> A **market segment** is a group of customers who have similar needs, attitudes, behaviors, and demographics, and can be satisfied by a single marketing mix.

His wife looks worried. "You're going after Sally's customers, Sam, and she is sure to retaliate. She will price her soap below your cost again, and put you out of business permanently. Even if you could sell as much soap as she does now, your production cost will be higher because you're making so many different kinds, each in small quantities."

Sam takes a moment to ponder her perspective. "You have a good point, Selma. Small batches are inevitably more expensive to produce than are long production runs. Setting up for each batch will take time and cost money. Moreover, each soap will require special ingredients that I will need to purchase in small quantities, raising my costs even higher. However, I will be able to lower costs somewhat with **economies of scope**, by sharing basic ingredients across my different soaps. Nonetheless, the fact remains, my costs will be higher than Sally's. But I'll make up for it by pricing my soap higher than hers."

> When you **save** on production costs by sharing ingredients and **processes** across different products, you achieve an **advantage** known as **economies of scope**.

Selma looks perplexed. "Sally makes a good bar of soap, Sam. Why will customers pay you more for yours?"

Sam replies, "Once consumers discover how suitable my soap is for their particular needs, they will not want Sally's all-purpose soap anymore. Then, what good will her high quality be? Her soap tries to be everything to everyone. As a result, it does not really satisfy anyone, despite its quality. Because my soaps will be more suitable for each segment, many consumers will be willing to pay more. If they are willing to pay more, how could Sally attract them by charging less? A price war will only hurt her profits without winning back her customers."

Selma seems satisfied with Sam's answer. Soon after, Sam launches his line of personal soaps at premium prices. Sally seems unperturbed, since Sam's prices are higher than hers. Moreover, her soap is an all-purpose soap, which she believes is more practical for her customers. "Who will want to buy 5 different soaps for one household?" she asks.

Meanwhile, Sam creates separate ads for each of his soaps, and places them where customers from each segment will see them. Even though kids and teens might never buy soap themselves, he advertises to them too, knowing that to obtain their preferred soap, they will influence the family soap decision-maker, whether Mom or Dad.

Before long, Sam's advertising starts to work, and Sally's soap sales start sagging. "This is silly!" she says to herself. "My soap is superior!" But as the weeks go by, she cannot deny that her business is facing a crisis.

Sally Gets Emotional

One day, she finds herself sobbing over a soap sample. "Why am I so emotional about soap?" she asks herself. "I'm emotional about it because I started the whole soap industry, and soap has made me successful. Soap is my life!" Recalling happy memories of her soap success, she dozes off in her chair, and dreams of soap, and success, and emotions.

> **Functional benefits** are the practical advantages of a product.

When she awakes, two words come into her mind: Emotions and soap. She thinks to herself, "Sam has segmented the soap market, and now he sells a different kind of soap to each segment. But he emphasizes just the **functional benefits** of his soaps, not the emotional benefits. I can segment the soap market too, as Sam has done, and I can create special soaps for each segment. But I can do more. I believe I can get people to feel *emotional* about soap. I can create ads and packaging that imbue my soap with emotional undertones, to help women feel more feminine, and men feel more masculine. My baby soap ads will evoke maternal feelings in mothers. And my teen soap ads will inspire feelings of peer approval and social confidence. These emotional benefits, added to my soaps' functional benefits, will increase the value of my soaps to consumers. People will buy my soaps not just to get clean, but to feel good about themselves too. Sam is not an emotional person, so he won't figure out what I'm up to it until it's too late. This is how I'll get my customers back."

Sure enough, Sally's new line of emotional soaps proves popular with consumers. Not only does she win back many of her former customers, but they show such loyalty and enthusiasm that even she is surprised.

Sam is puzzled by the appeal of Sally's new soap line. "Soap is certainly not what makes a man a man, or a woman a woman," he says to himself. "My soaps get you clean, they smell good, and they are suited to different kinds of skin. Those functional benefits alone should be enough." Nonetheless, it is clear that Sally has successfully segmented the soap market, and has tapped into consumers' emotions to strengthen her dominance of the soap industry.

Sam knows he is in a corner. Reluctantly, he starts redesigning his packaging and advertising to enhance the emotional appeal of his soaps. But he knows he will need to do more than that. He will need to trump Sally's emotion-based advantage, in order for his business to have any chance of survival.

Sam thinks to himself, "I have segmented the soap market. I have formulated each of my soaps to meet the special needs of each segment. I have also differentiated my soaps from Sally's original all-purpose soap. But now she has launched a new soap line that is really quite similar to mine, weakening my product differentiation.

And her pricing is also very similar to mine, which only compounds the problem."

"Sally has launched a frontal attack against my soap line, from a dominant market position. If I respond with price cuts, I am sure to lose, because her manufacturing costs are far lower than mine. What else can I do?"

He thinks about how Sally started as the only soap maker in the valley, selling her soap out of her own store. Without any competition, there was no urgency to distinguish her packaging, or establish a strong brand name. However, once rival soap makers started opening their own soap shops in town, the need arose for a stronger brand identity. She started imprinting the words, "Sally's Soap" on each bar, to create the impression that her soap was special.

Later, to expand her business, she started selling her soaps to independent soap and toiletry shops, located in the towns and villages scattered across the valley. This represented a milestone in her business, because from then on, she was selling to consumers with whom she was not personally familiar. Thus, she could no longer count on her own personal selling skills to establish and strengthen customer relationships. Instead, she improved her packaging and advertising, in order to strengthen her **brand**.

> Defined broadly, a **brand** consists of a product, along with its packaging, name, logo, functional and emotional benefits, and any supplementary imagery – such as advertising imagery – that is commonly associated with the product. In other words, a brand consists of everything about a product that customers find meaningful.

With the introduction of her new line of emotional soaps, Sally has created separate sub-brands, each with its own personality, for different segments of the market. For example, her Spring Flower  soap for women is sold in flowery packaging, and is supported by suitably feminine advertising. Her Buffalo River soap is positioned for men, with packaging and advertising based on a rugged outdoors theme. Each brand personality is created to assure the target customers that the particular soap is suitable for their own personal use.

Sam Searches for a Strategy

"Superior customer satisfaction is what drives soap success," Sam says to himself. "And to satisfy customers, you need to understand their needs. Some customers can tell you what they want, but most cannot. So I always try to imagine what my customers might like to have. Then I produce it. Staying close to my customers helps me understand their unspoken needs, and innovate successfully." And this is why, even though most of his soap is now sold through independent soap retailers, Sam continues to operate his own soap shop in Latherville. He wants to interact directly with his customers, and try to better understand their point of view.

To Sam's own surprise however, his next marketing strategy will not be based on product innovation, but on an exclusive relationship with a powerful new retail chain. Until now, the people of the valley have normally purchased their necessities at specialized shops, each carrying a narrow range of products. A typical shopping trip might entail a visit to the butcher, the baker, the produce store, and the soap store, for example.

But this all starts to change. An entrepreneur named Gary has realized that consumers are wasting a great deal of time by visiting so many individual stores in this manner. He is convinced that by making all their purchases in a single store, consumers could save time on each shopping trip. So he opens the first general grocery store in the valley, stocking a wide variety of goods for convenient one-stop shopping. His store quickly becomes successful, and soon, a Gary's Grocery store can be found in every neighborhood throughout the valley.

Gary's success has caught Sam's attention. Noticing that Gary does not carry any soap in his stores, Sam believes he has stumbled upon an opportunity. "If I can discover why Gary does not sell soap, perhaps I can convince him that he should," Sam thinks to himself. So one day, he pays Gary a visit and asks him, "Why do you not sell soap in your stores, Gary?"

"Not enough shelf space," is Gary's reply. "It seems everybody in the valley makes one thing or another, and they all want me to sell their products. My shelves have become so crowded, I've had to start charging each manufacturer a **slotting allowance** for shelf space. I could stock your soap, but I'd have to charge you." The word *greed* crosses Sam's mind, but he stifles any comment. Gary continues, "We need to generate a dependable profit from every square foot of our retail space. Every time we put a product on our shelves, we take a risk that it might not sell quickly enough to pay for the space it occupies. We're in a low margin business, and can't afford to take risks like that. So when we ask manufacturers to pay slotting allowances, we are really asking them to share in our risk. If their product doesn't sell, then at least the slotting allowances will have covered some of our costs. If the product does sell well, then the manufacturers can easily recoup the slotting allowances from their profits."

> The increasingly global economy has made an abundance of goods available to retailers, resulting in a shortage of shelf space. This has prompted some retailers to charge manufacturers a fee, or **slotting allowance**, for shelf space for their products. Slotting allowances compensate retailers for risking scarce shelf space on low-margin products. They also reflect a shift in the balance of power away from manufacturers and in favor of retailers in recent years. This has resulted from consolidation in the retail industry, as large, powerful national chains have gained market share. The legality of slotting fees is uncertain.

Gary's position is starting to sound a bit more reasonable to Sam. In any case, Sam believes that the benefits of distribution through Gary's Grocery outlets will far outweigh the cost of the slotting allowances. In particular, Sam is hopeful that Sally's customers might switch to his soap line if he makes it conveniently available in all of Gary's grocery store outlets. Consumers could save a great deal of time by purchasing their soap along with their groceries in Gary's stores, rather than making a separate trip to a soap store to purchase Sally's soap. So Sam agrees to pay Gary's slotting allowance fees, on the condition that he will be Gary's exclusive soap supplier. The deal is sealed with a handshake, and Sam's soap sales soar.

The Power Shift

Sally is furious. With the success of Sam's soaps in Gary's grocery chain, more and more of the customers who used to buy her soap at the independent soap shops no longer bother coming. Instead, they have switched to Sam's soap, purchasing it conveniently at their local Gary's Grocery outlet.

Having secured shelf space in a powerful new **distribution channel**, Sam seems to have gained an unbeatable strategic advantage. There is a price to pay, however. Sam's soaps have for some time been sold by the independent soap retailers. But these independent retailers are losing sales, as their customers increasingly purchase Sam's soap more conveniently in Gary's new grocery chain. Feeling betrayed by Sam, most independent soap shop owners now refuse to sell Sam's soap at all. Instead, they put their full support behind Sally's soap. But with sharply declining customer traffic, they are fighting a losing battle. One by one, they close their shops permanently.

> **Distribution intensity** is the extent to which a product is widely available from retailers or distributors.
>
> **Distribution channels** consist of the distributors, retailers, agents etc., that help make a product conveniently available for customers to purchase.
>
> **Channel conflict** arises when the firms feel that they are not being fairly compensated for selling a product, either because their rivals have an unfair advantage, or the product is too widely available.

While a few independent shops still carry Sally's soaps, they too are closing. Sally is quickly losing the **distribution intensity** that is necessary to ensure convenient availability of her soaps for consumers. Desperate to regain access to her customers, Sally arranges a meeting with Gary.

"I have always had the best-selling soaps in the market," she says to Gary. "That's because I make the highest-quality soaps in the entire valley. Moreover, customers just love my advertising. If you want happy customers, you'll need to carry my soap."

"Sally, my deal with Sam is exclusive," Gary replies. "I can't sell your soaps. Besides, I am extremely short of shelf space. I would have to charge you slotting allowances, as I do with all my other suppliers."

"That's okay, Gary. I'll pay whatever slotting allowances you need to charge," replies Sally, hoping Gary will somehow forget his exclusive deal with Sam.

But Gary intends to drive a hard bargain. "I appreciate your offer, Sally, but I do have an exclusive agreement with Sam, and I don't easily go back on my word." He pauses, and then continues, "My only complaint with Sam is that he's not ... flexible. For example, I've been looking for a manufacturer to make a line of soaps under our own **house brand**, but Sam says he's too busy. Almost thirty percent of our sales consist of our own house brand products, including Gary's coffee, Gary's breakfast cereals, Gary's dairy products, and so on. We want to expand the line to include soaps."

Sally's heart sinks as she realizes what Gary wants. "Gary is hoping I will manufacture soap at a low cost to be sold under his house brand. And then he'll sell his house brand soaps at a low price, undercutting my regular line of soaps. Is this the price I have to pay to sell my soap in his stores?" Sally wonders.

As a soap industry pioneer, Sally is a proud person. Faced with Gary's unyielding demands, she feels humiliated, and wishes she had never bothered meeting with him at all. But she is desperate, and Gary's grocery chain is her last hope. "Gary, if you will sell my regular soap line, then I'll agree to manufacture your house brand. But that's on the condition that you will allow me to be your exclusive soap supplier," Sally demands.

Gary sighs, and starts shaking his head slowly. "Sally, I can't give you an exclusive," he says, "My customers like Sam's soaps, and I'm not going to force them to buy yours."

Sally stares at him for a moment, and then looks down at the floor. She feels defeated, but decides to try one more ploy. "Okay, Gary, I'll do it your way. But I cannot pay any slotting allowances. And I want our agreement in writing."

A once-powerful manufacturer encounters growing retailer power.

"I can't help the slotting allowances, Sally. They're a fact of life in my business. But I will put our agreement in writing, if that's what you want."

Determined to extract one concession or another, Sally continues, "Gary, your customers will be thrilled to find my branded soaps in your stores. My soaps are the most popular in the valley. Moreover, I'll manufacture your house brand soaps at such a low cost, that no one will have any hope of competing with you. I am the only one who can do this for you."

"Well actually," Gary chuckles, "Larry Lightfoot came by the other day with a proposal, and…"

Sally cuts him off. "Larry Lightfoot makes laundry liquid. He doesn't know how to make personal soaps as I do. And his manufacturing costs are higher, so you'll pay more for his house brand product."

Gary knows she is right, but he denies it anyway. "You're wrong on that point, Sally. But I have to admit, you're one determined person, and I like that. Perhaps I can waive the slotting allowances this time. I'll do it as a favor for you. But I'm going to put my house brand soaps on my shelves right beside your and Sam's soap lines. I have to do it. My customers deserve a choice. That's the way we operate here."

"Alright. We have a deal then," Sally replies, hoping to renegotiate the shelving arrangements at a later date. As she reaches out to shake Gary's hand, she feels relieved to have reached an agreement. But she is also disconcerted by his unyielding bargaining tactics. "How has this retailer become so powerful?" she wonders.

As she walks away from his office, she thinks to herself, "Gary's retail chain is by far the largest we've ever seen in the valley, and he has no serious rivals to keep him in check. With the proliferation of products of all kinds these days, shelf space is scarce. Manufacturers have become desperate to retain access to their customers. Gary owns the scarce resource: The hottest retail shelf space around. He holds all the cards."

Then her thoughts drift to her present situation. "Now that I've negotiated some shelf space for my own product line, I'll have a chance to win back my customers from Sam. He'll never be able to match my quality. And he'll also have to compete with the low-end soaps I'm going to make for Gary's house brand. Time for justice!"

Meanwhile, on the outskirts of town, Sam is laboring in his barn, working on a secret new chemical formula for a substance he is planning to call ... *shampoo*.

Chapter 2

Envision a Bright Future for Your Firm

Have you ever noticed how some people seem quite content to live from day to day, while others are always dreaming up plans and pursuing ambitions? Which approach is better? For an individual, you could argue it either way. But for a company, there really is no choice. All the employees in a firm need to understand where the company is headed, so that they can work together.

To communicate your company's direction, you can create a written vision statement and a mission statement. Your **vision statement** should describe what you would like your firm to become at some point in the future. In contrast, your **mission statement** explains essentially how you will operate your business to achieve your vision.

What Is Your Mission?

Ideally, you mission statement should communicate your values, your purpose, your standards, and your special capabilities. These four ingredients can help make your mission statement clear and complete.[1] However, in the real world, these four ingredients are not always found in company mission statements. In fact, real company mission statements take many diverse forms. Some are only a few sentences long, and others extend over several paragraphs. Some firms seem to combine their vision and mission statements, while others have no published mission statement at all. Here are some examples of typical mission statements:

- University of Cambridge: "The mission of the University of Cambridge is to contribute to society through the pursuit of education, learning, and research at the highest international levels of excellence."
- Musgrave Group of Ireland: "The Group's mission is to create exceptional added-value from food businesses that are different and better, and to share the value created with shareholders, employees, customers and the community at large."

Though your employees may have an intuitive grasp of your intentions, a written mission statement can help them become more consciously aware of how you want your firm to operate. And it can help them perform more effectively as a team. It can also communicate your positive intentions to your customers and shareholders.

Take a moment now to write out a mission statement for your own company. See if you can succinctly explain your company's values, purpose, standards, and special expertise. Write your mission statement in a manner that will inspire both your employees and your customers.

Next, try to express what you stand for in a nutshell – in a mere handful of words. For example, "Tasty pizza delivered fast", or "Innovative websites that help companies build their brands". Encapsulating the bare essence of your mission, this kind of slogan, tag line, or mantra can be easily advertised – and easily remembered by your customers and employees.

As business conditions change, you might need to modify your vision and mission statements occasionally. But be careful not to change them so often that your employees and customers become confused.

Your company vision and mission statements can help you envision a bright future for your business. The rest of this book explains how strategic marketing can help make your vision a reality.

Let's Speak the Same Language

The imprecise use of marketing terminology can cause confusion. To avoid that, let's define some basic marketing terms.

- First, what is a **market**? A market consists of all the people who want to buy a product. But that's not all. They also need to be able to afford it. And the product needs to be available for purchase.[2]
- What is **market size**? Market size is normally measured by the quantity or dollar value of products that are likely to be sold in a particular year.
- What is a **product**? In this book, the term "products" should be understood to mean "goods, services, experiences, events, persons, places, properties, organizations, information, and ideas".[3] Each of these can be marketed in much the same way as tangible goods are marketed. But there are exceptions. For example, *service* marketing can differ from *tangible product* marketing in some important respects, as noted in this book.
- What is **marketing**? Marketing is the process of planning and executing programs to create value for your customers and for your company.

How Marketing Can Minimize Your Risk

For most businesses, financial risk is unavoidable. Fortunately, marketing can help you minimize risk. That is because marketing is externally oriented. It involves continually monitoring your customers and competitors, and staying alert to any threats and opportunities that your business might face. This can help you steer your business away from unnecessary risks, and toward profitable opportunities instead.

Risk is the danger that harmful events might occur in the future. For example, an expensive marketing program could prove ineffective, resulting in financial loss. If you could see into the future, you could avoid risk entirely. You could foresee which marketing programs would be unprofitable. While you might not think it's possible to see into the future, most people regularly anticipate the future to some extent in the course of their daily lives. For example, when you see thunderclouds forming, you know from experience to expect rain, and so you can carry an umbrella to avoid getting wet. You have learned from experience that certain patterns of events can forebode danger, or promise opportunity. The same is true in business. Certain sequences of events tend to recur. By recognizing them and anticipating the resulting circumstances, you can better prepare yourself for whatever challenges and opportunities may arise.

The *product life cycle* (PLC) is an example of a commonly recurring pattern of events in business. If you are aware of its typical progression, you can prepare your business for the challenges and opportunities that normally accompany each of a PLC's stages. For example, if you are aware that your PLC is transitioning from the *growth* stage to *maturity,* then you can expect your sales growth to taper off, and you can modify your business plans accordingly. You can also expect that rivals who were previously struggling to keep up with growing demand, may soon be free to turn their attention to stealing market share from you. Armed with this advance knowledge, you can organize your resistance, and take steps to retain your customers, before it's too late. This is one example of how an external orientation and a knowledge of marketing can reduce your business risk.

Marketing research can help you monitor your business environment. But marketing research is not the main topic of this book. Instead, this book will help you learn to anticipate the kinds of scenarios that are likely to emerge in your market. And you'll learn to formulate suitable marketing strategies, to make the best of your situation.

How Marketing Increases Your Risk

As noted above, there are several aspects of strategic marketing that can help you reduce your risk: observing, recognizing, analyzing, and predicting. But the actual implementation of strategies *increases* risk. This is because there is no way to know for sure in advance what the outcome of your strategies will be. While your strategies might result in greater sales and profits, you can also lose your money if your strategies fail.

Even after you have implemented your strategies, you may still be uncertain about how effective they have been. This is because your customers and rivals are exposed daily to innumerable, diverse influences. How can you be sure, even after the fact, that it was your strategy that made the difference, and not some other factor? Statistical analysis might yield some insights, if you have the requisite technical skills. Typically though, the complexities of a normal business environment will at least partially obscure the cause-and-effect relationship between your strategy and any particular result.

This uncertainty can lead some managers to be skeptical about the value of marketing. They might argue that any marketing spending that does not generate immediate verifiable results is wasteful. Their motivation to cut marketing spending can be even greater when the economy is slow and budgets are tight. Ironically, a time of economic stagnation may be just when your products are most in need of marketing support for their survival. It may also be a time of opportunity for you, as other firms pull back on their own marketing budgets.

You may depend on your marketing programs primarily to generate *immediate* sales revenues. But steady marketing support over the long term can help strengthen your brand, building customer trust and loyalty. Moreover, a strong brand can serve as an effective defense against price competition.

Marketing spending is inherently risky, and so some waste is inevitable. Fortunately, a knowledge of marketing strategy can help you minimize your risk. This book will help you acquire that knowledge.

What Is a Marketing Strategy?

A marketing strategy is an approach to selecting customers and satisfying them in a competitive environment so that you can generate profits and achieve your company goals. Marketing strategies address issues like:

- Which customers and needs will you attempt to satisfy?
- How will you differentiate and position your products to appeal to your target customers?
- How will you price your products to maximize your profits and offer attractive value for your customers?
- How will you provide convenient product availability and sales support?

- How will you leverage efficiency, innovation, and customer relationship management to strengthen your position in the market?
- What offensive and defensive maneuvers will you make to achieve an advantage over your rivals?

Keep Your Strategies Confidential and Flexible

Unlike your publicly-proclaimed mission statement, you may find it advantageous to keep your marketing strategies private. This can give you the advantage of surprise. By limiting any knowledge of your strategies to the key personnel who will actually need to implement them, you can reduce the chance that your rivals will learn about your plans. On the other hand, if your firm is a market leader, you may find that by publicly announcing your strategies, you can favorably influence the plans of weaker rivals.

Whether you keep your strategies private or not, it can be a good idea to put them in writing, to avoid any chance of misunderstanding. But while your strategies may be written on paper, they should not be written in stone. In other words, they need to remain flexible and adaptable to changing circumstances.

As your strategies are translated into short-term tactics, you may start receiving feedback originating from your customers and front-line employees. Some negative feedback may come from disgruntled or anxious employees who are reluctant to deviate from their usual way of doing things. It's important to distinguish this kind of negative feedback from genuine market intelligence that indicates a change in your business environment.

Your business environment may change unexpectedly, due to unforeseen competitor responses to your marketing strategies. However, when faced with change, you can be ready to adapt your strategies as necessary, if you

stay open-minded and receptive to feedback. In a rapidly changing market, adaptability and continual innovation can be among your most important sources of sustainable competitive advantage.

Be Externally Oriented

Sally's soap success grew out of her home-made cleaning products hobby. That sounds like fun. Are hobbies a good way to get started in business? Sometimes. Stephen Wozniak started tinkering with electronics as a hobby in his youth. His hobby eventually led to the founding of Apple, Inc.

However, hobbyists can be at a disadvantage, if they focus their attention entirely on their hobby. In other words, you might say some hobbyists are *product-focused*, and lack the external orientation that is normally necessary for marketing success. Fortunately for Wozniak, he teamed up with Steve Jobs, who did have the necessary external orientation.

Of course, Wozniak and Jobs were very fortunate to be the right people in the right place at the right time. Their strengths were well-matched to the enormous latent demand for personal computers. But just as importantly, their success with Apple, Inc. grew from a combination of Wozniak's product focus, and Jobs' external market orientation.

These days, progressive companies expect all their employees to be externally oriented and dedicated to serving their customers. If you adopt this kind of customer-focussed approach, it may help your whole team work together to deliver superior customer value.

Brainstorm with a SWOT Matrix

What threats and opportunities do you face in your business environment? What are your firm's strengths and weaknesses? To assess your situation, there is a simple creative tool you can employ, known as a SWOT matrix. A SWOT matrix can be used to compare your internal company strengths and weaknesses with your external opportunities and threats. As you might have guessed, the acronym SWOT stands for strengths, weaknesses, opportunities, and threats.

Take a look at the SWOT matrix example that follows. Read the instructions for completing it before proceeding.

Generally, you'll get better results from your SWOT matrix if you complete it with the help of at least one other person. That's because two brains are often better than one. Pick a partner who has good business judgment, a healthy imagination, a sense of humor, and a strong interest in your business. Then, using Larry's SWOT matrix as a guide, complete the blank SWOT matrix in this book to analyze your own business situation. You might be surprised at how easy it is to generate strategy options using this method.

Keep in mind that in order to obtain the best possible results from your SWOT matrix, you will need to think flexibly. As an example, consider how Larry completed his SWOT matrix. He considered the soap price war a threat. But with a different attitude, he could instead have considered it an opportunity to eliminate his smaller rivals. Similarly, by using your own judgment and imagination, you may be able to discover a wider range of opportunities when working with your SWOT matrix. But remember that with so much leeway for personal judgment and imagination, a SWOT matrix is only a rough brain-

Soap SWOT Matrix	Strengths Larry has experience with soap R&D and manufacturing. Larry has acquired a good knowledge of consumer needs.	Weaknesses Larry's production costs are high. Larry's positioning is not focused. Larry's soap is not well differentiated from Sally's.
Opportunities There is a strong demand for soap for many purposes. Consumers may be receptive to more specialized soap products. Sally's positioning is not focused. Sally has not segmented the market. Some smaller competitors are abandoning the market.	*Strategies Matching Strengths with Opportunities* Create new cleaning products to serve unsatisfied market segments. Build a strong brand to protect the new products.	*Strategies Matching Weaknesses with Opportunities* Differentiate Larry's product from Sally's soap. Reposition Larry's product to appeal to poorly served segments. Match Sally's price increases, once the other small competitors have left the market.
Threats Sally has the dominant market share in the soap industry. Sally's production costs are very low. A price war is in progress.	*Strategies Matching Strengths with Threats* Devote more resources to market research and R&D.	*Strategies Matching Weaknesses with Threats* Discontinue Larry's present soap product.

This example SWOT matrix shows Larry's situation during the price war, before he has introduced his laundry liquid. To create such a matrix, Larry would first list his strengths and weaknesses, as well as the opportunities and threats he faces. Then he would try to think of strategies that would match his strengths with his opportunities. He would write those strategies in the middle square of the matrix. Next he would match his strengths with his threats, his weaknesses with his opportunities, and finally, his weaknesses with the threats he faces. He would list these strategies in the remaining squares, as shown.

Your SWOT Matrix

	Strengths	Weaknesses
Opportunities	*Strategies Matching Strengths with Opportunities*	*Strategies Matching Weaknesses with Opportunities*
Threats	*Strategies Matching Strengths with Threats*	*Strategies Matching Weaknesses with Threats*

storming tool. Don't depend on it for a precise, scientific evaluation of your strategic circumstances.

To get the most from your SWOT matrix, try listing even some strengths that you don't presently possess, but could perhaps attain with some effort. This might help you generate a broader range of strategic options. For example, in his SWOT matrix, Larry listed his soap R&D expertise as a strength. But what if he had added his *potential* R&D expertise with household chemical products? This would have helped him to imagine additional strategic options, such as the creation of new household products, including floor polish, paint, and air fresheners. Likewise for your own business, you can use your SWOT matrix creatively. This can help you identify profitable opportunities that you might not otherwise think of.

The fertility of your imagination will greatly influence the quantity and quality of strategies you will be able to generate with your SWOT matrix. When generating ideas, try to avoid being overly judgmental, as judgments can impede the free flow of creativity. If you like, you can write down all your ideas – even the impractical ones – on a separate piece of paper. Wait until you have completely run out of ideas before getting judgmental. Then review your list, and cross off any strategies that seem entirely unrealistic, or just plain silly. Next, transfer your most promising strategies to your SWOT matrix.

While a SWOT matrix is commonly recommended as a component of periodic marketing plans, it can actually be used as a brainstorming tool at any time, especially when your business circumstances are changing.

In the process of completing the blank SWOT matrix in this book, you have matched the internal elements of your business with your external environment. The purpose was to generate some useful strategies. Did you think of any? If not, be patient; you will get better at it, as you explore this book.

On the other hand, perhaps you have found that the internal and external elements in your SWOT matrix are not very well matched. If so, how could you make them more compatible? Can you change your environment? That would seem unlikely, given the complex, unruly, and competitive nature of most business environments. Instead, you will probably find it more practical to focus on internal change, adapting your company to accommodate your chosen market. But before you start trying to change your company, be sure that you truly understand your market, and know which market segments you want to serve. Market segmentation is the topic of the next chapter.

Chapter 3

The Secrets of Successful Segmentation

Your present line of business has three basic parameters: your resources, the benefits you create with them, and the customers you satisfy. If we consider an example from daily domestic life, imagine that you are cooking a meal for some guests. In that case,

- Your *resources* would include your kitchen, your recipes, and your cooking expertise.
- The *benefits* you create would include the culinary delight and nutrition afforded by your cooking, and the pleasant ambiance your guests enjoy while they eat your meal.
- Your *customers* would be the people you entertain as your guests.

The resources you use, the benefits you offer, and the customers you satisfy, define the key parameters of your **served market**. They define the focus of your efforts, and the limits of your business. These parameters can be visualized as a triangle:

Key Parameters of Your Served Market

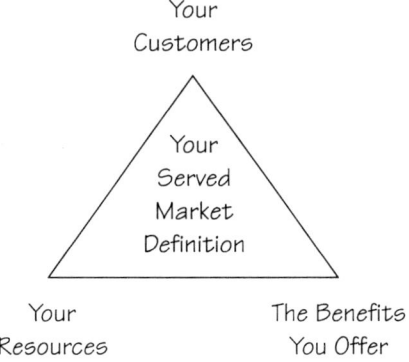

If you were operating a custom furniture store, you could apply the same model. You would use resources such as furniture designs, wood-working skills, and machinery, to create benefits like elegant, comfortable, functional furniture, to satisfy such customers as local residents and businesses.

Eventually, you might start wondering how to broaden the scope of your business. You might ask yourself whether there are additional opportunities and threats that you are not presently aware of. Exploring these could help your business reach its full potential.

To discover any unnoticed opportunities and threats, take another look at the resources, benefits, and customers that define your served market. For example, is your principal benefit merely furniture? Or could it be broader than that, including attractive environments for home and office? If so, perhaps you could expand your offering to include interior design services, for instance. Interior design services might help generate more furniture sales. They might also create a demand for accessories such as background music CDs, framed paintings, and artificial plants. And they might enable you to attract and satisfy more upscale customers.

Perhaps you could also expand beyond your local community, to target customers in neighboring towns and cities. Upon considering this broader market, you might discover that furniture shops in neighboring communities have been targeting customers in your local market for years, and have been unrecognized rivals all along. And you might also discover that some local interior designers have been purchasing exclusively from rival furniture shops, which is an advantage your rivals have been enjoying without your knowledge.

In opening your mind to a wider range of possibilities, you are exploring your **strategic market definition**. That's the official term, but unfortunately, it sounds like nondescript jargon, doesn't it? It's not very memorable. So let's use a catchier phrase instead. Let's call it your **opportunity triangle**. In the diagram that follows, you will see your opportunity triangle's key parameters. These include all the resources, benefits, and customers that could possibly be relevant to your business.

How broad should the parameters of your opportunity triangle be? That is something you must judge for yourself. The scope of your opportunity triangle will depend on which resources, benefits, and customers are realistically within the realm of possibilities for your firm. In contrast, your *served market definition* includes only the resources, benefits, and customers that fall within the *present* scope of your business activity.

Defining your opportunity triangle broadly will help you avoid marketing myopia. **Marketing myopia** is a term that means having too narrow a perspective when defining the scope of your business. If you suffer from marketing myopia, you will tend to miss opportunities – and fail to recognize looming threats. To avoid this, your

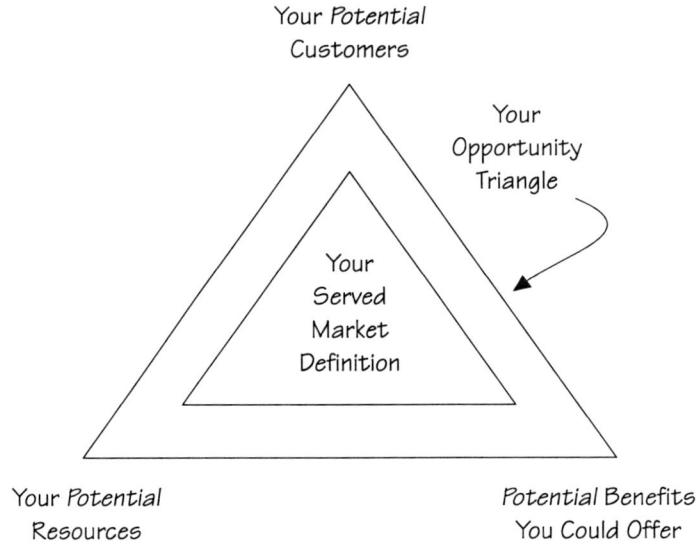

A broadly defined opportunity triangle can help you discover previously unnoticed opportunities and threats relevant to your business.

opportunity triangle should be broad enough to include all potential opportunities relevant to your business.

In each row of the following **opportunity table** you will find a brief description of a possible opportunity for the fictional furniture business. After looking over this table, take a moment to analyze your own situation. In the blank table that follows, list all the possible opportunities you can imagine for your own business.

One way to approach this task is to sit down with two or three friends – over a few beers, if you like – and write a list of your firm's present resources, benefits, and customers. Next:

Indispensable Marketing Strategies

Row	Name of Furniture Business Opportunity	Required Resources *Expertise & Assets*	Current & Potential Benefits *Products & Reputation*	Current and Potential Customers	Threats *Trends, the Economy, Your Rivals, etc.*
1	Expanded the existing furniture business.	Business name and logo. Retail space. Manufacturing and office equipment. Expertise in furniture production.	Furniture that offers comfort, functionality, and visual appeal. Helpful sales consulting and customer service.	Small businesses, and middle or upper-income individuals in the local and neighboring communities.	Intensified competition as rivals in nearby communities resist the expansion.
2	Interior design	Interior design expertise.	Solutions for clients' interior design needs.	As above, with emphasis on the more prosperous businesses and higher income individuals.	Competition from interior designers, some of whom may have greater expertise.
3	Decorative Accessories	Same as row one, with additional purchasing know-how, and knowledge of current decorating trends.	Same as row one, with emphasis on tasteful accessories instead of furniture.	Same as row one.	Competition from home decor shops, department stores, and big box retailers.

- Try to think of new *benefits* that you could create using your existing resources. Which customer groups would value these benefits?
- Try to think of additional *customers* you could serve. What benefits would they appreciate? Do you have the necessary resources to generate these benefits?
- Try also to think of additional *resources* that might be available to you. What benefits would these resources allow you to create? Which customers would value these benefits?

Before pursuing this discussion further, you'll need to remember what a marketing mix is. Your **marketing mix** consists of your product, its price, your advertising, and the channels through which your product can be purchased. Any group of people who are likely to be satisfied by a single marketing mix can be considered a *market segment*.

Now let's take another look at the hypothetical furniture retailer's opportunity table. If you look at the customers shown in the right hand column of Row #1, you will notice that they are comprised of several different kinds of customers. And different kinds of customers tend to have different needs. For example, your business customers will need office furniture, while home-owners will need household furniture. Since these customers are so different, they need to be considered separately, as distinct market segments. Each of these segments will need its own marketing mix.

Now, look at your own opportunity table again. Pick the opportunities that offer the most profit potential, and seem best suited to your capabilities. Cross off the rest. Then, for each of your chosen opportunities, ask yourself whether the target customers would likely be satisfied by a single marketing mix. If not, you will need to divide them

Row	Name Your Opportunities in This Column	Your Required Resources *Expertise & Assets*	Your Current & Potential Benefits *Products & Reputation*	Your Current and Potential Customers	Threats *Trends, the Economy, Your Rivals, etc.*
1					
2					
3					

further into homogenous segments, and create a separate marketing mix for each. For example, an appropriate furniture marketing mix for a high-income home-owner might include:

- Product: Swank, premium-quality furniture
- Price: High prices, consistent with high quality
- Channel: An exclusive, high-service retail outlet
- Promotion: Classy direct mail advertising.

Coarse Segmentation

Each dot on this perceptual map represents the product attributes that are considered ideal by an individual survey respondent. The four dot clusters indicate the needs of four different segments. Product X is positioned to satisfy all four segments, though it is not ideal for any of them. To purchase product X, the customers must compromise - in the direction of the arrows. They do so only because there are no alternatives.

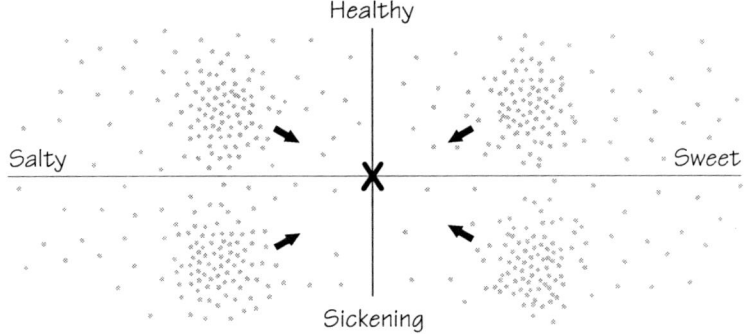

How Finely Should You Segment?

When you define a market segment, be sure that the customers within your segment are similar to each other in some respect. But how similar? No two humans are identical, and no two business customers are completely alike either. While one customer may be entirely happy with your marketing mix, another may be less so. The less satisfied customers must compromise their preferences to purchase your product. And so, if a rival firm offers a marketing mix that more closely suits their needs, your less-satisfied customers may switch.

For example, suppose you sell coconut cookies in supermarkets, and a rival starts selling similar coconut cookies with a little less sugar in health-food stores. In this case, any of your customers who shop in health-food outlets and prefer less sugar may start purchasing from your rival. So it seems, no matter how you segment your market, you will not be able to please everyone entirely. A rival who offers a different marketing mix may be able to entice some of your customers.

Finer Segmentation

Rival firms segment the market with products A, B, C, and D. They position these products to more closely match each segment's needs. As shown by the arrows, the customers purchase whichever brand offers the attributes they value most. As a result, product X loses market share.

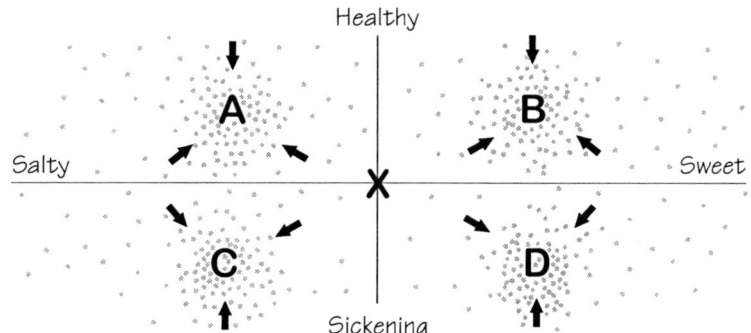

One solution to this problem is to segment more finely. In other words, you can divide your market into even smaller segments. To satisfy each of these smaller segments, you can offer variations of your marketing mix to suit each segment's particular preferences. For example, you could create your own low-sugar coconut cookies, and sell them through health food stores, to discourage potential rivals from doing the same.

However, as you segment more finely, you will have to produce your product in smaller batches. Because of this, you will lose economies of scale, and this will increase your costs. Your costs may be further increased by the complexity of managing a great many different marketing programs. Hence, you will be forced to charge higher prices, and your customers may balk at having to pay them. As well, if you offer your product in too many varieties, your customers could become confused.

Therefore, you should segment your markets finely enough to satisfy and retain your customers, but not so finely that your customers become confused and your prices are forced up to uncompetitive levels.

Another solution to this problem is a process known as mass customization. Like old-fashioned tailor-made clothing, mass-customized products are created to the specifications of individual customers. Because they are customized, these products require less customer compromise. But *mass*-customized products have a big advantage over traditional tailor-made items: They are much more affordable, thanks to some efficient new production technologies. Dell is an online computer retailer that has demonstrated the technical know-how, marketing finesse, and large scale of operations required to succeed with a mass-customization strategy. Using their advanced production technologies, they have learned to satisfy individual customers' needs, while keeping their prices competitively low.

But mass customization will work only if your customers are willing to make the necessary effort to educate

> **High-involvement products** are items that involve consumers a great deal during purchase or use. This is typically because these products have a significant impact on consumers' lives, as they are used frequently, or they are particularly interesting or socially significant, or they are complex and expensive. Being so important or risky, these products tend to attract close attention during the purchase process.

themselves about your products, and make informed choices about which items or components to purchase. This can be a lot of work. In fact, most customers will be willing to make a greater effort only for **high-involvement products**, such as computers and cars. Otherwise, customers may find it simpler to have a salesperson recommend what to purchase.

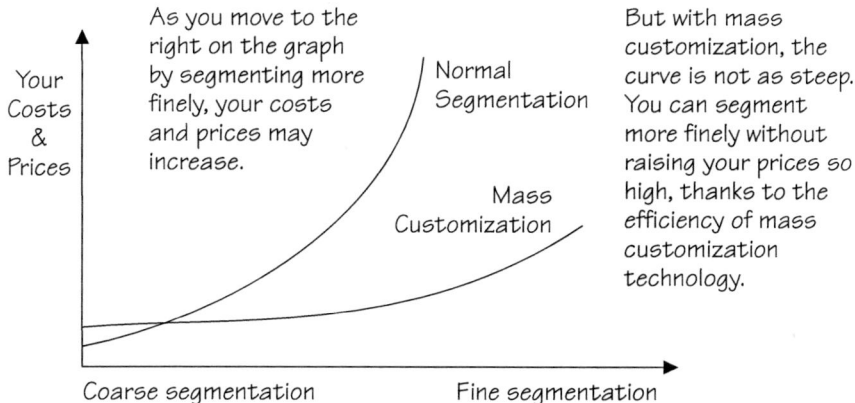

How Finer Segmentation Affects Costs and Prices

If you want to offer mass customization yourself, you will probably need to make a substantial investment in advanced production technologies and web site programming. To recover such a large investment and earn a profit, you will likely need access to a large market segment, so that you can achieve a high volume of sales. Given these obstacles, it is no surprise that most firms still depend on more traditional approaches to market segmentation.

Which Segmentation Variables Are Best?

One of the challenges you will encounter when segmenting a market is that there may seem to be countless different ways to group your customers. To simplify your task, you should segment first according to your customers' needs. Once you have identified a segment whose needs you are capable of satisfying, try to define the segment more precisely. Try to segment your customers according to their *psychographics*, which includes their values, interests, and opinions. You can reflect their psychographics in your advertising, so that they will feel that your product reflects their values. Also segment your customers according to their *behavior*, including what magazines they read, where they shop, and on what occasions. Their behavior will dictate the media in which you should advertise, the channels through which you should sell your product, and the timing of your promotions. For the same purpose, you should determine their demographics, including their location, income, and language. If the task proves too complex, consult a marketing research firm for assistance.

While business markets are quite different from consumer markets, you should still start the segmentation process by considering your business customers' needs. Next, segment according to such variables as location, industry, and business culture.

Are you selling an established item? If so, you may also need to segment your market according to whether or not your target customers have already purchased your product. Existing customers may need reminders to repurchase. In contrast, potential customers might need more education about your product, along with incentives to try it. If your existing and potential customers require different advertising messages, you should treat these two groups as separate segments.

What Makes a Segment Attractive?

Generally, you should target only attractive segments that are well-matched with your firm's strengths, as the following table[4] indicates:

	Unattractive Segments	Attractive Segments
Your Superior Capabilities	In these segments, serve only the customers that are worth your effort.	Prioritize these segments.
Your Inferior Capabilities	Leave these customers for your rivals.	If possible, improve your capabilities to serve these customers.

Are you interested in expanding into new market segments? If so, you will likely want to target whichever segments offer the most profit potential. Among the factors that can indicate a segment's profit potential are its size and growth rate.

For a rough estimate of a segment's size, you can use the **chain ratio method**. This entails making a succession of percentage calculations. Here is a simplified example of how to calculate the demand for cell phones in a hypothetical market that is not growing:

How to Estimate Segment Size Using the Chain Ratio Method

Total population	300,000,000 individuals
Percentage of population owning a cell phone	10%
Number of cell phones in use	300,000,000 individuals x 10% = 30,000,000 cell phones
Expected lifespan of each existing cell phone	Each cell phone is used for 3 years on average
Annual demand for replacement cell phones – assuming no growth in demand	30,000,000 cell phones divided by 3 years = 10,000,000 cell phones per year.

Why is a growing segment usually more profitable? Here are two reasons:

- If you sell products that are purchased repeatedly – such as food items – many of the customers in your market will develop steady habits and strong brand loyalties. Hence, customers who are already loyal to a rival's brand will prove difficult and costly for you to attract. So you will find it less costly and more profitable to target first-time customers who have not yet become loyal to your rivals' brands. Since first-time customers are more common in growing markets, growing markets tend to be more profitable.

- To capitalize on segment growth, you will normally need to enter the segment early in the product life cycle (PLC). This is when almost all growth occurs. By entering early, during the PLC growth stage, you are likely to end up with a larger market share. This should help you achieve economies of scale, which will also have a positive impact on your profitability.

However, growth can sometimes also occur later in the PLC. For example, the mature market for baby diapers could suddenly grow, as a result of an increase in pregnancies and child births. But in most cases, the best time to enter a market is during the high-growth early stages of the PLC. As long as your segment keeps growing, you will find it easier to build your business.

Another important factor that can influence segment attractiveness is the stability of demand. If you target a segment that is subject to seasonal fluctuations in demand, you may need to find other uses for your idle capacity during slow seasons. For example, hotels located in seasonal tourist destinations can try to attract business conventions, in order to fill their rooms when tourists are absent. Small souvenir shops may simply close up, until the tourists return.

Intermediaries are companies that sell another firm's products. Examples include wholesalers, distributors, agents, retailers, and dealers. If you must sell through numerous intermediaries in order to reach your market, then your distribution channels are considered to be **fragmented**. If just a few large firms dominate distribution in your market, then your channels are considered to be **consolidated**.

In addition, your segment's profit potential can be greatly influenced by the kinds of customers, competitors, suppliers, and distributors that you will need to interact with, as follows:

- A segment will not offer much sales and profit potential if your prospective *customers* are likely to take your product without paying for it. For example, many software and entertainment firms have found their markets less attractive, now that some consumers download digital intellectual property over the internet without paying.
- The segment will be less attractive if it is targeted by too many strong and aggressive *rivals*. This is even more true if you lack any special advantage, whether it is the lowest production costs, superior quality, or outstanding service. If you have no special advantage in a particular segment, you may be forced to compete on price. But if you don't have the lowest costs, competing on price could eliminate your profit margins.
- Your business could be further complicated by *suppliers* who are unreliable or too expensive. Some suppliers may even be unable to serve you at all, if they are already heavily committed to serving your rivals. And service providers such as government institutions, postal services, and royalties agencies, can be heavily bureaucratized and unresponsive to your needs. Circumstances like these can make a segment less attractive.
- An additional challenge can be posed by *distribution channels* that are **fragmented**. If this is the case, you'll have to sell your product through hundreds or thousands of small **intermediaries**, which could involve considerable effort. If your channels are not

fragmented but are instead **consolidated**, you may need to sell through large powerful retail chains that bargain your prices down and make onerous demands.

Considering all these challenges, it's a good idea to investigate carefully, so that you can target whatever segments seem to offer the most profit potential, while avoiding those that are likely to prove problematic.

Segment Entry Strategies

Once you have identified the most promising segments in your market, you will need to decide on the order in which you will enter them. You can enter just the one segment that offers the most profit potential. Or you can enter multiple segments at once, if you have sufficient resources. Otherwise, you can start with a single segment and gradually enter others in a **sequenced entry strategy**. This might allow you to make inconspicuous progress, without seeming to be a threat to your rivals. Alternatively, you could target the entire market in a **mass-marketing strategy**. Mass marketing is suitable for undifferentiated products that have broad appeal, like milk, nails, or cardboard boxes. Another option would be a **mass customization strategy**, offering products that are uniquely suited to individual consumers' needs on a mass scale.[5]

Like any new strategy, your segment entry plans can meet resistance from within your firm. Some personnel may resist because they have learned to profit from the status quo. Others may have valid concerns that your segmentation strategy is flawed. For instance, if you normally sell fashionable apparel at premium prices, and you're planning to enter a budget-conscious segment, there may be some justifiable apprehension that your strategy could damage your firm's reputation.[6] However, if all reasonable concerns can be addressed, then entering a new segment may prove well worth your effort. Penetrating a new segment may enable your firm to exploit growth opportunities, or avoid aggressive rivals, or adapt to a rapidly-changing business environment.

Choosing which market segments to serve is an important strategic decision for your business. You should reconsider this decision periodically, even if your products are already established. Occasional review of your segmentation strategy can enable you to identify newly emerging segments, or to reconsider segments that you had previously overlooked. Even an hour or two of occasional analysis and brainstorming might yield ideas or discoveries that could have a profound impact on your business. While you're at it, review your opportunity table, to be sure that your opportunity triangle is still sufficiently broad.

How Switching Costs Can Lock You Out

If you enter a segment that is already dominated by a large, entrenched rival, you may be in for a fight that you cannot win. An established rival may have superior economies of scale, a deeper knowledge of the market, and popular brands. On the other hand, if your product is distinctively positioned and functionally superior, you may have a competitive edge. But even then, your success is not guaranteed.

For a number of reasons, your target customers may be unwilling or unable to switch to your product. One possible reason is that they may prefer your rivals' products because of their lower price, despite their inferior quality. Or they may be exposed to a high level of rival advertising and sales effort that is beyond your capabilities.

> Certain factors can make it difficult for customers to switch from one brand to another. These factors are known as **switching costs**. They can include having to learn new software, or discard a previous investment, or abandon points earned in a customer loyalty program.

In some situations, your target customers may be faced with **switching costs**. They might be bound by contract to continue buying from their present supplier. They may be concerned that adopting your product would be too risky, or too disruptive, or would require too much effort. For example, if you are selling complex accounting or production software, an established business customer might need to endure weeks or months of disruption while switching to your product. Or your customers may prefer your rivals' products because they are compatible with a wide variety of other complementary items. For example, it was partly the broader selection of movies – complementary items – available on VHS video cassettes that resulted in the demise of the competing Betamax video-cassette format. Switching costs like these can impede your market penetration.

On the other hand, if your products are already established in the market, the tables may be turned. You might be able to create your own switching costs to retain your existing customers and block your rivals.

Hide in a Niche

Entering a large segment can sometimes enable you to achieve a high sales volume, and earn substantial profits. However, large segments can attract large rivals, and large rivals can be tough competitors. Therefore, if you are fortunate enough to be the first to enter a large segment, then you should move quickly to secure a dominant position. You should try to establish customer loyalty, achieve the lowest costs, and discourage other potential rivals from entering.

> A **niche segment** is a segment that is too small to be of interest to large companies, but substantial enough to be profitable for a smaller firm.

But what if the large segments of interest are already occupied, and you have no special advantage over your rivals? In this case, entering a small **niche segment** may prove to be a more fruitful strategy. Targeting a niche segment can enable you to gain a foothold in a market without having to face excessive competition.

Among your initial objectives, you should try to achieve a "first-mover" advantage. Try to develop innovative products and technologies, tailored to your segment. As well, try to acquire in-depth customer knowledge and build lasting customer relationships. Then, if the market eventually grows enough to attract larger rivals, your firm will already have a substantial head start.

The early market for personal computer software is a good example of niche growth opportunities. At first, this market seemed too small to attract large firms. And so, in the absence of overwhelming competition, small startups like Microsoft and Apple were able to develop their technology and establish dominant industry standards, such as Windows® and the Apple operating system. As the software market grew, it was their first-mover advantage that enabled firms like Microsoft and Apple to become entrenched, and retain their leading market share.

Whether or not your niche actually grows, it will nevertheless provide an opportunity to incubate your business in an environment that is not too competitive. If you can succeed in one segment, you will be better prepared to enter others, gradually building your strength.

Profit from Radical New Ideas

Sometimes, it may be possible to bypass established rivals in a large segment, by offering a radically new solution to a customer need. But your radically new product may be at a disadvantage if it seems so unfamiliar that it confuses your customers. This was the case for early personal computers and software. They took years to catch on, because they seemed unfamiliar and intimidating to most people.

By contrast, Starbuck's unique premium coffee experience caught on more quickly because coffee was already a favorite drink for so many people. However, Starbucks' exotic coffee concoctions and their distinctive restaurant ambience were a significant departure from traditional coffee marketing. This allowed Starbucks to grow without facing entrenched competition. By marketing a familiar product in a radically innovative way, Starbucks was able to swiftly set up an international network of outlets, and establish a widely recognized brand name.

Similarly, YouTube offered Internet users a radically new way to experience something already familiar: entertainment and news videos. What was radically new was the opportunity for individuals to easily showcase their own video creations to the whole world. This resulted in an enormous variety of unique and personal video creations being made available for viewers to watch whenever they wanted. With the launch of the YouTube website, the community of video contributors and viewers quickly snowballed to a critical mass that rendered any subsequent rivals irrelevant. Now that YouTube is established, it is the *size* of the community that attracts so many viewers and contributors. The more members there are in the community, the more valuable the community is to its members. This *network effect* is the basis of YouTube's most important sustainable competitive advantage.

However, in getting started, it was their radically new approach to a familiar product that enabled both YouTube and Starbucks to achieve domination of their respective market segments so quickly. And crucially, they did not need to dislodge any large, entrenched rivals in order to succeed.

If It Looks Too Good To Be True ...

If you are fortunate enough to have discovered a large, wide-open market segment that has not yet been penetrated by rivals, you may be on the threshold of a golden marketing opportunity. But look before you leap! If your segment is not presently served by any rivals, then ask yourself why that is so. If your rivals consider your target segment unattractive, then why should their reasoning not apply in your case?

They might consider your target segment unattractive because it is too small or too geographically remote. It may lack targeted media, like magazines, TV shows, or websites that would allow focused, cost-effective advertising. Your segment may lack appropriate distributors or retailers. It might be prone to lawsuits, or excessive government regulation. Or perhaps your rivals believe it would be impossible to erect barriers to protect the segment against entry by other competitors, and as a result, price competition might be too intense.

If any of these concerns are valid, how is your company better positioned than your rivals to overcome these challenges? Do you have a radically new approach?

Do you have any unique expertise? Do you have access to information that your rivals lack?

If you cannot uncover any reasons for your rivals' reluctance to seize the opportunity, it may be that they are presently distracted by other matters. Or perhaps they lack the necessary financial and human resources. Or they may consider the segment irrelevant to their long-term goals. Or conceivably, they simply do not appreciate the profit potential of your target segment.

If your segment entry strategy addresses every valid concern that applies to your situation, then the large, untapped market you have discovered may represent an opportunity of extraordinary promise.

Sell Your Product as a Branded Ingredient

Entering a new segment normally involves considerable effort and expense. But in some cases, you can penetrate a market more cost-effectively by riding piggyback on another firms' success. This can be done by selling your product as an ingredient or component in the other firm's products.

Normally, the brand name of an ingredient or component cannot be easily identified by consumers. For instance, a package of bread will not usually indicate what brand of flower was used to bake it. But some other ingredients or components do maintain their distinct identity, and can be recognized by the final consumer. These are known as **branded ingredients**.

For example, Intel CPU chips are recognizable components found in many personal computers made by other firms. They are recognizable because they are identified by the "Intel Inside"® logo and catchphrase on the outside of the computer. This ensures that consumers are aware of the Intel brand, even though they cannot see the CPU chip itself.

As another example, a famous brand of chocolate chips such as Hershey® might be prominently mentioned on a package of cookies, to enhance their appeal. Or a carpet manufacturer can differentiate their product by featuring a branded stain-resistant ingredient, such as StainMaster®. A packaged food company can advertise their use of a branded artificial sweetener such as Splenda® to highlight the low-calorie advantage of their food. Or a Shimano® derailleur can be prominently featured on a bicycle to emphasize its high quality. These are all examples of branded ingredient products.

Could your own product be used as an ingredient in products marketed by other firms? Is your brand name strong and distinctive enough to enhance the host product's appeal? Is your product well-matched with the host brand? Are your company values compatible with those of the host brand's firm? For example, if you support protection of the natural environment but the host firm does not, you may experience ongoing conflict over this issue.

If there is a good match between your firm and the host firm, then your product may be welcomed by them as a branded ingredient. And if the host product performs well in the market, then your own ingredient product will share in the benefits.

Alternatively, your product may be more suitable as a host brand itself, instead of being an ingredient brand. That is, another firm's ingredient brand could be incorporated into your product. This can enable you to add the ingredient brand's appeal to your own brand. However, if the same ingredient brand is eventually adopted by all your rivals, it may become a required feature for all products in your category, and will no longer be a source of distinctiveness.[7]

License for Profit

Licensing is a special form of ingredient branding whereby you allow other firms to reproduce your images, text, or music, to enhance their products. Disney's Mickey Mouse® character is commonly licensed in this manner. Other items, such as The Simpsons®, Sesame Street®, and Peanuts® cartoon characters are licensed for use with clothing, household items, and toys. Popular music is licensed for use on CDs, with cell phones, and in movies. Proprietary industrial technologies are licensed for use by firms that lack the technologies they need for their products.

One important advantage of licensing your products is that licensing can enable you to generate profits without the burden of having to manufacture or stock inventory. However, you will need to ensure that the quality of the host products supports the reputation of your brand. Any association of your brand with shoddy merchandise could degrade your brand image and damage customer trust. On the other hand, a relationship with a dependable licensee could earn substantial revenue for your firm.

If your company does not own intellectual property that would be suitable for licensing, you might consider becoming a licensee yourself. This can allow you to benefit from the appeal of well-known music or cartoon characters, or to offer the functionality of technologies developed by other firms.

Bypass Obstacles

Penetrating a market segment is typically a challenging task for any business. In some circumstances, the barriers to entry raised by your rivals may make the task so daunting that it hardly seems worth the effort. But before giving up, try to think of how you can circumvent any obstacles that stand in your way. For example, if the large greeting card retail chains don't have room for your line of art cards, try selling them in independent giftware boutiques instead. If the local restaurant trade is dominated by giant franchise operations, consider focusing your food service business on ethnic cuisine, home delivery, or catering. By looking for ways to circumvent any obstacles, you may well stumble on approaches to marketing your product that are superior to what you had originally intended.

Chapter 4

Position Your Product for Customer Trust

The phrase *strategic marketing* may evoke images of stealth, intrigue, and competitive struggle. By comparison, one of the foremost priorities of strategic marketing may seem rather mundane: customer satisfaction. But customer satisfaction is crucial for profitability. To earn profits, you must have sales, and to generate sales in the long run, you must have satisfied customers.

Listen to Your Customers

To satisfy your customers, you must first understand them. How can you learn more about your customers? One of the best ways is to interact with them personally. If you are targeting business customers, you may be fortunate enough to interact with professional buyers who are trained to evaluate products rationally and systematically. Try to encourage their feedback – and keep an open mind so that you can benefit from their suggestions. Listen actively and empathetically. If you show a genuine interest in their concerns, they will feel that their feedback is welcome. As you build rapport, they may open up and tell you more about their needs than they tell your competitors, giving you an important advantage.

Your salespeople need to understand this. If they are impatient to earn commissions, they may feel that listening and information-gathering are a waste of time. How then will they respond if a customer makes a critical comment about your product? If they brush off a valid criticism, they could miss an opportunity to help you learn more about your customers' needs.

> An **objection** is a reason given by a potential customer for not purchasing your product. A skilled sales person will try to overcome objections, not by dismissing them, but by solving any underlying problems and addressing any customer concerns.

Of course, many customer **objections** or complaints are simple matters that can be resolved, with some imagination and resourcefulness. Misunderstandings can be corrected. Anxieties can be assuaged. And special requirements can be accommodated. Skilled salespeople can distinguish between minor objections like these, and the kind of objections or complaints that arise from a fundamental flaw in your product. They understand that brushing aside objections or valid criticisms would convey a lack of genuine concern. This could damage your customers' trust, possibly motivating them to purchase from your rivals.

Instead, your salespeople should be trained to welcome customer feedback. They should understand that customer feedback can provide crucial insights that can help you improve existing products and develop new ones. Moreover, customers like to know that you take their concerns seriously. Many are eager to make a contribution and help you learn to satisfy them better.

Indispensable Marketing Strategies 73

A private moment ...

Smitten by peanut butter love, Gwendolyn confesses her deepest feelings of attraction and loyalty to her favorite brand.

Are They Emotional or Rational?

Because cost-effectiveness is a primary concern for business customers, their purchasing decisions tend to be carefully calculated. They cannot afford to be impulsive or emotional, as they must purchase responsibly, on behalf of their company.

In contrast, consumers cherish the freedom to purchase as they please, within the constraints of their household budgets. When purchasing entirely on their own behalf, they are more likely to make self-indulgent, emotional purchasing decisions.

Generally speaking, business purchasing decisions are made rationally, while consumer purchasing decisions tend to be made more emotionally.

To appreciate the implications of this for your business, imagine that you have just landed a new job. Your sole responsibility is to advertise a brand of beer. You are competing against nine other beers that are identical in all respects, including price. What should you do? (In reality, people disagree about whether beers vary in taste from one brand to the next. But in our story, the 10 beer brands taste exactly the same.)

Without any differentiation between the competing products, effective positioning would likely be your sole source of competitive advantage. Suppose then that you tried to position your beer as "the best beer". Would that give you an unbeatable advantage? Or would your competitors merely follow suit? The answer is, no, you would not have an unbeatable advantage. And your competitors probably would not follow suit either. If they all claimed to be the best, then none would have any advantage, as they would all be positioned identically.

Instead, each beer would likely claim its own unique benefits. This could give them an advantage over you, if their specific claims were more credible to consumers than your relatively vague claim to being "the best". What specific benefits could you then claim for your beer to distinguish it from its physically identical competitors?

Beer is often used as a social lubricant. That is because people gathering to socialize want to overcome their feelings of awkwardness, and want to feel socially at ease. Beer helps them relax and feel confident in those situations. Additionally, in social gatherings, a person's choice of beer is conspicuous. Perhaps by choosing the same beer as their friends, people unconsciously express a desire to share. They may also hold their beer as a token of membership in their social group. If this is the case, why not claim group membership and social ease as benefits offered by your beer?

However, if your beer becomes a symbol of membership in one social group, it will likely be rejected by other groups that have incompatible values. Therefore, you will find it advantageous to target a particular social group, to the exclusion of all others. After selecting a target social group – or market segment – you will need to expose your target customers to advertising that reflects their values, their social aspirations, and so on. Your advertising will need to demonstrate that, by consuming your beer, your customers could satisfy their emotional needs, as well as their thirst.

Upon witnessing the success of your marketing strategy, your competitors would probably target the remaining segments in a similar manner, modified to suit each segment. Thus each segment would eventually be served by a beer tailored to their respective emotional needs. Each segment would have a beer that they could consider their own.

Football Beer or Ballerina Beer?

As an example, suppose the advertising for one particular beer supports values agreeable to aspiring football players, while another beer celebrates the thirst of ballerinas. (Ballerinas won't normally admit to drinking much beer, but people who secretly aspire to being ballerinas no doubt occasionally yield to the temptation.)

How many self-respecting football players do you think would be caught dead drinking the ballerina beer? Zero? The two beers are physically identical, but for the football player, the positioning of the football beer offers emotional benefits: It's personality seems consistent with his athletic male self-concept, and with that of his peers too. Therefore this beer can serve as a comforting symbol of membership in his social group.

> **Cognitive dissonance** is a feeling of mental and emotional discomfort that results from having various beliefs or behaviors that conflict with each other.

In contrast, the personality of the ballerina beer would be too feminine for the football player. Drinking it would cause him considerable **cognitive dissonance**. Moreover, his friends might be offended if he adopted such an apparently feminine beer, and might even ostracise him as a result.

Given the very real social and emotional repercussions of drinking the ballerina beer, the football player would be very sensible to avoid it. Nonetheless, the special benefits of the football beer are only emotional and symbolic. There are no functional advantages, as both beers are physically identical.

Indispensable Marketing Strategies

If your beer were positioned as "everybody's beer", would the football player prefer it? Probably not. Your beer would offer only ambiguity. It would lack the reassuring sense of identity and belonging imparted by the football beer.

To compete with the football beer, you would be well-advised to target an entirely different segment of the market. Perhaps you could position your beer to appeal to people who consider female mud wrestlers or aristocratic gentlemen to be inspiring role models. Such individuals would tend to value your beer if it gave them a comforting sense of personal identity and group membership.

On the other hand, these particular segments might be too small to be worth pursuing. And you might have ethical concerns about persuading consumers to depend on alcohol as a social lubricant or for self-esteem. But the point is, you can position an undifferentiated product such as beer so that it offers distinct emotional benefits that are valued by a specific target segment.

Emotional decision-making is most obvious when consumers buy products that are distinctively positioned, but lack clear differentiation. The ten identical beers described in the previous story are a good example. They are undifferentiated in their taste and smell, and in their appearance when poured in a drinking glass. Consumers are unable to distinguish between their respective functional benefits – because there is no difference. Instead, consumers have only the beers' perceived emotional benefits on which to base their purchase decisions.

How Positioning Can Override Differentiation

Even when products are well-differentiated, emotions can still play a crucial role in consumer purchase decisions. Though a consumer may carefully compare a product's functional benefits, its emotional benefits may be what actually tips the scales in its favor.

Consider various models of cars, and how different their inner workings might be. These mechanical differences may seem incomprehensible or even unimportant to some consumers. As a result, consumers will sometimes resort to emotional decision-making.

For example, imagine a fictitious consumer named Carl, who is trying to buy a new car, without having any in-depth product knowledge. Even after he narrows down the possibilities by price, fuel economy, and friends' recommendations, he is still left with several acceptable models. Given that the inner workings of the cars are beyond his understanding, and that each model offers essentially the same perceived functionality and esthetics, how can he choose? The only remaining criterion may be his gut instinct. Since the advertising for one of the models features people similar to Carl, he feels that that model was designed for people like him. The car's positioning alone gives him a gut feeling favoring that model.

Once his emotional preference is established, he may concoct rational justifications, to persuade himself that his decision is logical. These *rationalizations* help him build the confidence he needs to act on his essentially emotional purchase decision.

In reality, he may have chosen a car that is mechanically inferior. In any case, since he cannot understand or appreciate the technical differences between the models he has considered, he has made his purchase decision emotionally. Most consumers would do likewise, when faced with product differentiation that they can neither comprehend nor appreciate.

Does this mean that all consumer car purchase decisions are entirely emotional? No. Generally, each consumer will seek his or her own ideal combination of functional and emotional benefits. But the less knowledgeable a consumer is about a particular product category, the more emotional his or her decision will likely be.

Brands Make Purchasing A Breeze

Imagine a person named Linda, standing in the aisle of a self-serve retailer named the Generic General Store. She is trying to choose from among five boxes filled with powdered laundry detergent. Each box is identical, except for its own printed list of chemical ingredients. Even with a degree in chemistry, Linda is not inclined to invest half an hour of her time reading these lists and evaluating the relative merits of the different products.

She instead decides to shop at a competing store named Brands Unlimited, where she again finds five boxes of powdered laundry detergent on display. But in this store, each product has a unique name, and a distinctive package design. Having previously been exposed to advertising for each of these products, she already knows which one she prefers, and can easily make a purchase decision.

In the second store, Linda's purchase decision was much easier, because she was able to select from among five distinctively branded products. But what exactly is a brand, and how does it facilitate consumers' purchase decisions?

A brand might be defined as a product's name or logo, and nothing more. However, that is not the way customers think of brands. When people say that their favorite brand of toothpaste is Crest® for example, they do not usually mean that they like just the logo. They usually mean that they are attracted to the entire brand experience – or most aspects of it – including the packaging, the advertising, and the product itself. For this reason, it is more useful to think of brands in broader terms.

It would also be incorrect to think of a brand as just a product. A brand is more than just a product, in the same way that a person is more than just a body. Much as you might know a friend by his name, attire, talents, and character, you also can know a brand by its name, packaging, benefits, and personality. A person's name is like a brand name. A person's signature is like a brand's trademark. Personal clothing is like brand packaging – except that we usually hope that people will change their clothing more often than brands change their packaging. A person's talents are like a brand's features and benefits. And in the same way that every person has a personality, brands may have their own personality too – some more than others. You'll find it most useful to think of a **brand** as a collection of all the aspects of a product that are meaningful to consumers.

Two types of brands are commonly recognized: **functional brands** and **image brands**. *Functional* brands offer mainly *practical* benefits. For example, computer printers are typically marketed as functional brands, emphasizing practical benefits like speed of printing, quality of color, and operating cost. In contrast, image branding is more appropriate when the functional benefits of competing products are difficult to distinguish. For example, since one beer may taste much like another, marketers tend to rely on supplementary imagery to position their beer brands with emotional benefits. Hence, they are considered image brands. However, most brands derive their appeal from a combination of both functional and emotional benefits, though they may emphasize one or the other.

A third kind of brand, known as **experiential brands**, focuses on the customer experience, rather than on product ownership. In other words, experiential brands are more service-oriented. But their appeal still depends on functional and emotional benefits. For example, experiential branding is utilized by businesses as diverse as hotels and rock bands. The functional benefits of comfortable accommodations are offered by hotels, while the emotional benefits of exciting music are offered by rock bands. Therefore, you may find it most useful to think of experiential brands as functional or image brands that happen to be service-oriented.

Benefit from Branding

How can branding give your business a competitive edge? Mainly through brand awareness, trust, and emotional bonding. These three factors are closely connected. Your customers need to be aware of your brand before they can trust or like it. But some brands can be trusted even if they are not liked. You may trust insurance companies and banks, even if you don't especially like them.

Branding will put a recognizable face on your product, giving it a unique and memorable identity. This will help your customers get acquainted with your brand, and learn to trust it. It will enable them to recognize and choose your brand when they feel a need for the benefits it offers. This is how branding helped Linda choose between five different laundry detergents. She chose the brand that she recognized and trusted.

To promote emotional bonding, you can give your brand an appealing personality. For example, cars are often endowed with personality traits in their advertising.

A car can be portrayed as having a defiant attitude, in order to appeal to people who resent the status quo or want to emphasize their individuality.

As previously noted, one purpose of branding is to build trust in a product – or to plant seeds of doubt about a rival product. As an example, consider the "I'm a Mac – I'm a PC" television commercials for Apple computers. These commercials personify PCs as socially awkward, incompetent, and pathetic. Most viewers would rather identify with the Mac, as he projects a self-assured, capable image. Moreover, the interplay between the two personalities highlights the Mac's purported advantages in a non-technical way. This builds trust in Mac computers, while undermining trust in PCs. The characters' humorous antics also help break down our resistance, making it easier for us to change our point of view. And we might feel that Apple must be a pretty cool company to have thought up such clever commercials. Thus, without really delving into the technical merits of either product, these commercials may emotionally bias our judgment in favor of Mac computers. Without branding, this kind of emotional bonding and trust would be impossible.

Brands Can Reduce Perceived Risk

The flip side of trust is perceived risk, and that is something that most customers prefer to avoid. Customers may perceive a risk that your product might not function correctly, or may be of poor quality. If that turns out to be the case, your customers would have to waste their time complaining about it or requesting a refund. If a refund could not be obtained, then they would have lost the money they spent.

Financial risk is also commonly perceived when dealing with service providers, such as building contractors, automobile repair shops, and lawyers. The reason for this is that the amount of effort required to provide the service is often unknown in advance, and so uncertainty about cost of the service can remain a source of anxiety until the final bill is presented. Service businesses should therefore take steps to assuage their customers' concerns by explaining in advance what work might need to be done, and how much it might cost.

In addition, customers may worry that a product might poison them, electrocute them, burn them, or cause some other personal injury. A restaurant meal could make them sick, an electric room heater could cause a fire, or a car could roll over. Customers may be worried that a computer game could cause their children some psychological harm.

A purchase may also turn out to be a source of embarrassment. Examples include botched plastic surgery, or a fancy sports car that constantly breaks down. Embarrassment can even result if your customers' friends tell them they have paid too much.

No matter what you have for sale, your customers may perceive some risk in purchasing it. By branding your product, you can reduce their perception of risk. Customers tend to trust branded products more, because they believe that companies stake their reputation on their brands, and will stand behind their brands to support their reputation. But this can be a double-edged sword: A trusted brand that fails to satisfy can cause consumers to feel greatly disappointed, betrayed, and resentful.

Push and Pull Strategies

A manufactured product that is branded effectively will appeal not only to your customers, but also to your wholesalers and retailers. They prefer strong brands because they *sell* better. Moreover, if your brand is popular with consumers, a retailer who refuses to carry it might risk losing business to rivals who do carry it.

When you motivate consumers to purchase your brand from your retailers, you are utilizing what is known as a "pull" strategy. In other words, your brand's popularity will generate consumer demand that will "pull" your product through your distribution channel.

By contrast, a "push" strategy entails focusing your efforts on persuading retailers to carry your product, display it prominently, and make an effort to sell it. With exposure to your brand at the point of purchase, consumers will hopefully be motivated to buy your brand on impulse, or in response to your retailers' sales effort.

Whatever combination of push and pull influences you prefer, having a strong brand may be crucial to your success. The strength of your brand may even be the deciding factor that determines whether you will be able to secure any shelf space at all in today's increasingly crowded retail stores.

How Brands Are Born

How can you build a strong brand? Start by identifying an unsatisfied customer need. Then create a product to satisfy it. For example, if you know that people need their homes and yards cleaned up, you could start a franchised trash removal service, as the firm "1-800-GOT-JUNK?" has done.

Alternatively, you can work the other way around. You can invent a product or technology first, and then try to find a need that it can satisfy. 3M's Post-it Notes® started with the accidental invention of a very weak glue that the inventors initially had no particular use for. It was only sometime later that a marketable use was found for the glue as an adhesive for sticky paper notes. However, not all inventors are so fortunate. It's quite possible to spend a great deal of effort inventing products that nobody will ever want. So commercial success will be more likely if you identify an unsatisfied customer need first, and then create a product to satisfy it.

After creating your product, you will need to name and package it attractively. You will likely need to advertise your brand over a length of time before your customers will recognize it and understand its positioning. Since they will not be able to keep up with frequent changes in positioning, you should keep your positioning fairly consistent and stable. To help accomplish that, you should establish and reinforce your positioning by presenting a consistent brand image across all your advertising media. For example, you should ensure that the message and graphics on your website match what is shown in your magazine, newspaper, and television advertising. You should also avoid large price swings that could confuse your product's perceived value.

Among the most important ways to protect your brand is to ensure that customer complaints are handled effectively, to preserve your brand's goodwill. In addition, if rapid advances in technology or changes in style are common in your industry, then you should keep working to improve your product, to maintain an up-to-date image. And you should consider pursuing legal recourse against product counterfeiters, so that your customers can purchase your brand with confidence.

Brand Equity Is Worth the Investment

If you brand your product effectively, it will likely command a higher price than it would if it were not branded at all. The premium your customers are willing to pay – simply because your product is branded – is a measure of your brand equity. Your **brand equity** is the value added to your product by branding, beyond the value of its functional benefits alone. The benefits you reap from your brand equity may include a higher selling price and greater customer loyalty.

To see how this might work, imagine that you sell a line of fruit pies. Your customers prefer your brand of fruit pies partly because the packaging displays a friendly grandmother image. This image evokes pleasant associations and suggests old-fashioned natural ingredients. As well, your pies have become famous as a result of your frequent advertising. Your brand's positive associations and fame inspire enough trust that your customers are willing to pay more for your brand, and are more loyal as well. In the long run, the higher profits that result from this may pay back your investment in branding many times over.

Position Your Brand Distinctively

In many ways, branding a product entails endowing it with humanlike qualities. Your brand will need a name, a distinctive appearance, and perhaps a personality as well. However, there is an important difference between people and brands. While a person can be in only one place at a time, a mass-produced branded product can be available simultaneously on thousands of store shelves around the world. Being widely available in unlimited quantities, any two brands that are similar may end up competing relentlessly everywhere for the same customers. Such intense competition can drive their prices down, cutting into profits.

This is one reason why products that are very similar, like beer, tend to be positioned with distinctly different emotional benefits. With different emotional benefits, they can appeal to different market segments. In this way, they may be able to avoid the destructive effects of head-on competition.

Even brands that are not mass-produced can benefit greatly from unique positioning. For example, theme parks and holiday resorts commonly cultivate their own distinctive positioning, to draw customers from around the world.

Whether your product is mass-produced or not, you should position it distinctively to avoid head-on competition, and to occupy a special place in your customers' minds. But where is that special place? To find it, you will need to find a place in your customers' minds that is not yet occupied. You will need to identify needs that are not presently being satisfied. To simplify that task, you can use a *perceptual map*.

How to Use Perceptual Maps

A **perceptual map** is a two-dimensional representation of how customers perceive competing products in a market. For example, the following perceptual map shows how consumers perceive two fictitious brands of ice cream. The Blinkbat product is perceived as extravagant and high in fat, while Aunt Mildred's product is considered natural and low in fat. From perceptual maps like this one, you can gain a better understanding of how consumers distinguish between two or more brands.

Ice Cream Brands on a Perceptual Map

A perceptual map like this can show how customers distinguish between two brands.

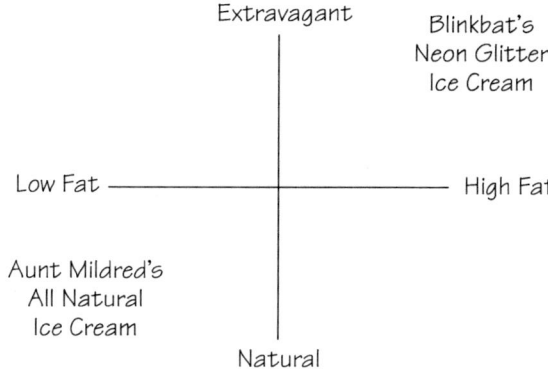

You can also use perceptual maps to compare how different customers have described ideal products that they wish for. This can help you discover unsatisfied market segments. For example, after the introduction of the Football Beer, and before any other beers were introduced, a competing brewery hired a market research firm to conduct a survey of beer drinkers. The brewery wanted to discover how closely the Football Beer matched its target segment's ideals. They also wanted to discover any other segments that were still unsatisfied.

The researchers uncovered two principal criteria used by consumers in evaluating beer. One of these criteria was whether or not the beer was considered masculine or feminine. The other criterion was whether the beer was perceived to be elegant and refined, or rugged and earthy. The researchers designed a survey with questions that participants answered by circling a number on a scale from one to ten. Obtaining quantitative results in this manner enabled the market researchers to plot the survey responses on a perceptual map.

Each dot on the following perceptual map represents the attributes that were considered ideal by an individual survey respondent. Most of the responses fall into one of four clusters of dots. These clusters represent market segments. The Football Beer's positioning, marked with an X, appears in the center of one of these clusters. This X indicates how customers perceive the Football Beer, on average, while the dots indicate their individual beer preferences. Since the X is aligned with a dot cluster, we know that it has been accurately positioned to appeal to that particular segment. The remaining three segments are as yet unserved, and the market researchers have named them as shown.

From this perceptual map, it is apparent that those who prefer a rugged, masculine beer are satisfied with Football Beer, whereas those who prefer an elegant, feminine beer are still thirsting for something more suited to their tastes. The survey respondents who have been dubbed "mud wrestlers" and "aristocrats" also remain unsatisfied. The researchers therefore suggested that the brewery launch three new beers to satisfy these three segments. The brewery proceeded as advised, starting with the successful launch of Ballerina Beer.

A perceptual map can be used to compare the positioning of your products – or your firm itself – with that of your rivals. Or it can be used to compare your own brands with each other. You can even use a perceptual map to compare your own personal positioning with that of your friends and associates.

To quickly create a perceptual map for brainstorming purposes, you can use your own *intuitive* estimates of how customers perceive the brands in your market. However, when it comes to making final decisions, it's best to rely on perceptual maps that are based on actual customer survey data.

Beer Preferences on a Perceptual Map

The dots represent individual customer preferences. The areas where the dots are most concentrated mark the four beer consumer segments. These segments have been humorously named as exaggerated personality types. The X represents the actual positioning of the football beer.

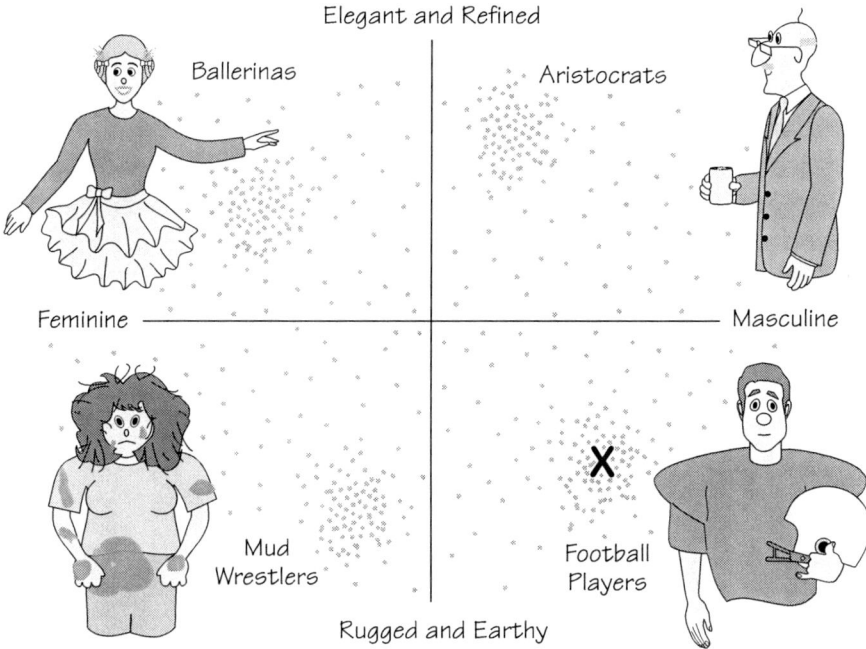

In order to position a product uniquely, you should consider not only how it compares with competing products, but also how it compares with your own products. You can start by plotting their positioning on a perceptual map. If you discover that two of your products are positioned in a very similar way, they may in fact be confusing your customers. If that is the case, you should consider combining your two brands into a single brand. Not only will a single brand be less confusing, but it will also require less marketing effort and expense.

Perceptual maps can help you ensure that your brands are positioned distinctly. To keep your brands even more organized, you can also make use of a brand hierarchy diagram. The following fictional narrative illustrates how.

Gunther's Galactic Spaceship Company

Gunther Groetzner, an astrophysicist and spacecraft engineer, has entered a new industry: The manufacturing and marketing of pollution-free, ultra-quiet recreational spacecraft. With two wildly popular models already on the market, Gunther is eager to launch a variety of new products, before his competitors can gain a stronger foothold in the market. A methodical person by nature, Gunther starts by organizing his existing and planned brands into the following brand hierarchy diagram:

The Galactic Brand Hierarchy

Company Brand: Galactic

Family Brands: SpaceJet, LightSpeed

Product Brands: LibertyOne, FriendShip, Duet, PointMan, ExecuTeam

The dotted lines indicate proposed brands.

As shown above, Gunther's brand names are organized on three levels. At the top of the hierarchy is the *company* brand name, Galactic, known for precision German engineering. Below that are the *family* brand names, including SpaceJet, which is widely associated with high quality recreational spacecraft. On the lowest level are the *product* brands. Among them is the LibertyOne, a sporty single-seater spacecraft aimed at adventurous young males who enjoy short excursions around the solar system on weekends. This product brand name is synonymous with youthful independence, freedom, and adventure.

In contrast, the FriendShip is a larger spacecraft, with room for six adults to travel in comfort. This brand name is associated with sophisticated socializing occasions for the wealthy.

Gunther believes that his brand associations are clear enough that his customers can intuitively understand which of his products are appropriate for their particular needs.

How to Organize Your Brand Hierarchy

Using a pen and a sheet of paper, draw a hierarchy for your own products. Beside each brand name, write the associations you would like it to have. If you don't yet have any products, use some imaginary ones, or else use another company's existing products.

The number of *levels* in your brand hierarchy may differ from the number of levels in the Galactic brand hierarchy. If your firm is like most, your hierarchy will have two or three levels.

As well, some firms clearly associate their company brand with their products, whereas other firms don't. For example, while you may know which company manufactured your car, you may not be aware of which company manufactures your laundry detergent.

Whatever the structure of your brand hierarchy, the point of drawing it is to ensure that your brands are logically organized, and will not confuse your customers.

Avoid Confusing Your Customers

What is so bad about confusing your customers? Some companies seem to believe that they can benefit from customer confusion. Examples of this can be found in the consumer electronics industry. Have you ever shopped for consumer electronics, and found it difficult to compare products, because their specifications are not listed completely? Typically, it is the inferior specifications that are omitted.

Manufacturers of inferior products tend to omit their weaker specifications because they do not want their products to be directly compared with higher-quality alternatives. It seems they hope that at least some customers will become confused enough to purchase their products, despite their inferior quality. Perhaps a limited degree of confusion can be advantageous for weaker products. This can be even more so if the manufacturer compensates for the confusion by emphasizing emotional benefits instead. The widespread use of this tactic would seem to attest to its effectiveness.

Generally though, confusion repels customers. People have an innate need to make sense of the world around them, and confusion frustrates that need. If your product or brand hierarchy makes no sense to your customers, then they are likely to turn their attention elsewhere.

Why then do some advertisers announce new products with only a partial disclosure of their features? Even Gunther used a vaguely worded ad to introduce the LibertyOne prior to its official launch. "Interplanetary flight? Sure beats doing your homework! The LibertyOne. It's almost here!" the ads proclaimed, leaving much unexplained.

The reason why Gunther and other advertisers sometimes use this approach is that partial disclosure can pique customer interest. As long as the ad offers a credible and enticing promise of satisfaction, customers may be prompted to seek more information, or least wait in suspense. Partial disclosure can be effective, as long as it does not completely confuse your customers.

If you leave your customers completely confused about the nature of your product and how it stands to benefit them, then you will lose their interest. Deluged with advertising and overwhelmed with choices, today's customers don't have the time or inclination to investigate products that seem incomprehensible and irrelevant.

How can you avoid customer confusion? Position your brands clearly. Start by learning how your customers make sense of your products. Usually, both logic and emotions are involved, though often without your customers' awareness. By learning to understand your customers' reasoning and emotions, you will be able to position your product more accurately and effectively. The following section explains how.

Products Need to Belong

When customers first encounter your product, they need to understand what it is. You can use words to tell them, of course, but that will succeed only if your product seems to be what you say it is. For example, if you, as a consumer, see an ad for products that appear to be small, circular, flat, sweet, crunchy, edible baked goods, how would you categorize them? Chances are, you would recognize these attributes as typical of cookies. Even if the manufacturer calls them something else, like paperclips or golf balls, you will probably think of them as cookies, because they have typical cookie attributes.

These typical attributes are known as **points of parity**. Points of parity are attributes and imagery that customers normally associate with products in a particular category. If your product lacks points of parity with any established product category, then your customers may be unable to understand what your product is. For example, if you attempt to sell some new software by explaining only that it is fast and easy to use, your customers will be mystified. They will not have enough points of parity to categorize your product and make sense of it. Once you explain that your software will enable them to create and print electronic documents, and that it includes a spelling checker and a thesaurus, you will have provided enough points of parity for them to understand that you are offering word-processing software. Points of parity are especially important for innovative financial and high-tech products, because customers can initially find them confusing.

At this point, you might be wondering how you could possibly categorize a new product that is so revolutionary that it does not seem to belong to any category at all. There is a solution to this conundrum: Relate your product to a category that has at least some relevance. For example, if you were responsible for marketing the very first personal computer, you might categorize it as a kind of electronic calculator. You might also categorize it as an electronic hobbyist's do-it-yourself kit. Similarly, the very first airplane could be categorized as a means of transportation, competing with cars, trains, and hot-air balloons. The very first telephone could be categorized as a means of communication, competing with telegrams and horseback couriers. What's important is to give consumers a point of reference, so that they can relate your product to a category with which they are already familiar.

Products Need to Be Special

After your customers have mentally categorized your product, you will need to show them how it differs from your rivals' products in the same category. Your customers will need exposure to attributes and imagery – known as **points of difference** – that set your product apart from its competitors.

For example, once your customers realize that you are selling word processing software, you will need to point out how your product differs from other word-processing programs. If you explain that your word-processing software can translate from Chinese to Lithuanian at the touch of a button, or that it can create documents by reading your mind, then you will have provided some points of difference that will help your product stand out.

As another example, Gunther's LibertyOne advertising emphasizes creature comforts, affordability, and adventurous entertainment. These are points of difference that distinguish his product as a personal recreational spacecraft, rather than a space vehicle designed for scientific exploration. He also associates the LibertyOne with precision German engineering imagery, as a point of difference with respect to the flimsy, unreliable personal spacecraft marketed by his rivals.

Note the distinction between product differentiation and points of difference: Differentiation refers to features that actually make a product different. By comparison, points of difference are the distinguishing characteristics that consumers *mentally associate* with a product. For example, a car may be differentiated from other models by its internal mechanics – which are ignored by less-sophisticated consumers – and its exterior design – which is not ignored. In addition, its advertising imagery may have persuaded consumers that it also has a special personality – which is a point of difference, but not a real differentiating feature. The car's personality is a point of difference that exists only in consumers' minds. In contrast, its design is a real product attribute that exists both in customers' minds and in reality. This "core product attribute" is both a differentiating feature and a point of difference.

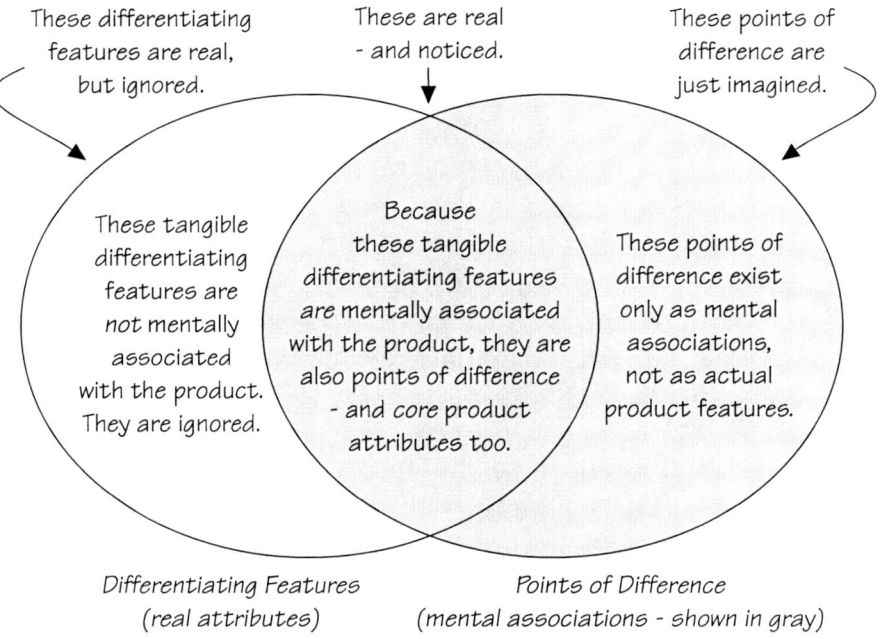

Be the First Thing They Think Of

In your customers' minds, your points of parity and points of difference locate your product within their existing network of mental associations. Your points of parity ensure that your product is correctly categorized. And your point of difference help customers distinguish your product from similar items. Once located in your customers' mental network, a brand can be readily recalled.

This is exactly what Gunther wants to happen in the minds of his potential customers. He has drawn the following need-satisfaction map. It shows how customers' mental associations could enable them to recall his product when the appropriate need arises. He hopes that the next time his potential customers consider making a recreational spacecraft purchase, the LibertyOne's points of parity will ensure that it is included in their **consideration set**. At the same time, however, Gunther wants the LibertyOne to be associated with precision German engineering, as a point of difference, to help it stand out from competing items in its category.

Need Satisfaction Mental Association Map

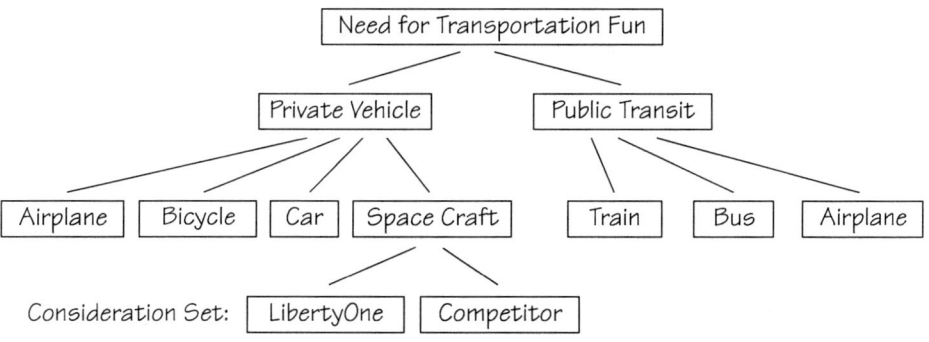

Customers should be able to locate the LibertyOne in their minds through a series of associations, from their initial need, through successively narrower product categories, to the product itself. Points of parity can help ensure inclusion in their consideration set. Points of difference ensure distinctiveness.

> A **consideration set** – or evoked set – consists of all the brands that a customer remembers and considers purchasing upon experiencing a particular need.

It is both your product's points of parity and its points of difference that allow your customers to remember it when they wish to make a purchase. It is especially your product's points of difference – or its distinctiveness – that can cause your customers to prefer it over competing alternatives. By enabling your customers to compare your product with its competitors, your points of parity and points of difference establish your product positioning in their minds.

Your Brand Will Provoke Judgments

Your customers can experience your product's points of parity and points of difference both rationally and emotionally. That is, your customers can make rational judgments about your products, and have feelings about them.

It will tend to be your product's core attributes that provoke rational judgments. Your **core attributes** include your product's features, functional benefits, esthetics, and price. For example, if you are selling cookies, their features might include healthy ingredients and stay-fresh packaging. The functional benefits could include a satisfying taste, easy digestion, and a long shelf life. The esthetics might include your cookies' appetizing appearance and your attractive package design.

What are your own brand's core attributes? Are they likely to be judged favorably by your customers?

Your Brand Will Evoke Feelings

Besides favorable judgments, you will want your customers to have positive feelings about your brand. One way you can connect with them emotionally is via the **supplementary imagery** shown in your brand's advertising. This imagery can suggest possible users, usage occasions, your brand's personality, its heritage, and its social status.

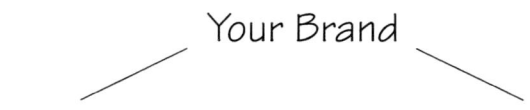

Core Attributes

- Features
- Functional Benefits
- Esthetics
- Price

Supplementary Imagery

- Typical Users
- Common Usage Situations
- Brand Personality
- Symbolism
- Social Context: Associated Companies, Countries, Distribution Channels, Brands, Spokespersons, User Communities, Events, Reviews, and Awards

Core attributes tend to be evaluated rationally, whereas supplementary imagery is often evaluated emotionally. This varies by customer, product, and circumstance.

For example, a TV ad for your cookies could show a likely group of *users* – young people for example. They could be eating your cookies while engaged in a casual social interaction – which is a possible *usage situation*. Your advertising might also make your cookies appear to have a particular *personality*, whether playful, sophisticated, or traditional. And if your cookies were originally created in an old Boston bakery, then including mention of their *heritage* in your advertising could add to their distinctiveness and charm.

In addition, your cookies might represent *values* such as health-consciousness or good parenting. They might have a special *social status* conferred upon them by association with a prestigious retailer – if they are sold in classy department stores, for example. Social status can also be imparted by association with a famous spokesperson, or a sponsored event.

What supplementary imagery do your customers associate with your own product? Does your supplementary imagery evoke positive emotions?

Important, Memorable, Credible Positioning

Your product's core attributes and supplementary imagery define your product's positioning, in much the same way as your points of parity and points of difference do. You can refine your brand's positioning by selectively emphasizing whatever attributes and imagery you believe are most important. But how can you decide what to emphasize?

Start by identifying all the other brands that might compete with yours. Include indirect competitors from other categories. For example, if your product is fruit juice, you might need to compete not just with other fruit juice brands, but also with soda pop, bottled water, beer, and anything else that quenches thirst. In this case, all the brands your customers consider for quenching their thirst are referred to as their *consideration set*. You should try to ensure that your brand is included in their consideration set, so that they will consider your brand for purchase.

To be included in their consideration set, your advertising should emphasize points of parity that will establish your brand's relevance to your customers' needs. You should also emphasize your most appealing points of difference. For example, if you are selling a computer printer that offers superior color accuracy and printing speed, you should emphasize whichever of these two attributes your customers value most.

In some cases, you may be able to convert weak attributes into strengths. For example, with their slogan, "We're only number two. We try harder", Avis highlighted their second-place ranking in the car rental industry as a credible motivation for superior service. By doing the unexpected – proudly proclaiming their inferior industry ranking – and by converting this weakness into a strength, Avis created a striking and memorable point of difference. Their slogan also attempted to reposition their competitor – the market leader – as complacent, and likely to take customers for granted.[8]

Avis' slogan illustrates ideal positioning in several respects. For one thing, it was striking enough to make a *memorable* impression. If instead it had been so bland or ordinary that their customers could not remember it, then it would have had no enduring impact. In addition, Avis' positioning claimed superiority on an *important* attribute – outstanding service. If instead their positioning had been focused on an attribute that seemed unimportant to their customers, then their brand would likely have been ignored. As well, Avis was a respected brand, making a *credible* promise – that as the industry underdog, they would try harder. If instead their reputation had been previously tarnished, or if their brand had already been positioned poorly, then they would have needed to make a special effort to re-educate their customers and reposition their brand. Or if their claim had seemed unbelievable, customers would not have trusted it. For best results with your own brand, be sure its positioning is important, memorable, and credible.

Your positioning decision will be crucial to the success of your brand. You'll stand a better chance of making a good decision if you take a few moments to write it down, as a **positioning statement**. This will help you think it through carefully. And it may also help you avoid misunderstandings both within your company and among outside consultants. Your statement should define your *target market*. It should also list the *points of parity* necessary for membership in your brand's product category. It should list the *points of difference* that promise superior customer satisfaction. And it should explain how your brand's core attributes and supplementary imagery will elicit positive judgments and feelings from your customers.

Position Your Brand Clearly

You have learned that your customers have an innate need to make sense of the world around them. To avoid frustrating that need with confusion, you need to position each of your brands distinctively. They should be positioned distinctively both with respect to each other, and with respect to your rivals' brands.

You can position your brands by utilizing points of parity and points of difference. But the points of parity and point of difference associated with your product are also core attributes or supplementary imagery. The following matrix illustrates how this applies to the LibertyOne:

Positioning Recreational Versus Scientific Spacecraft

Positioning

	Core Attributes	Supplementary Imagery
Points of Parity:	Rocket engines & space travel capabilities.	Advertising images of the LibertyOne flying through space.
Points of Difference:	Creature comforts and leather upholstery not found in scientific spacecraft.	Advertising images of personal space travel, freedom, and adventure.

Differentiation
(The gray cell only)

As you can see from the above matrix, your product's attributes will be the focus of a customer evaluation process that involves two overlapping dimensions. Your product will be categorized, distinguished from its competitors, judged rationally, and responded to emotionally. The more important your product is to your customers, the more intensive their evaluation process will be. Once the process is completed, a favorable purchase decision will hopefully be at hand.

Now construct a similar matrix, and list your product's attributes in it. In positioning your product, you can decide which of its core attributes to emphasize, entirely at your own discretion. And of course, the choice of which supplementary imagery to associate with your product is a matter for your discretion as well.

How Services Differ From Physical Products

Throughout this book, the word "products" is used broadly to include both *physical products* and *intangible services*. Most marketing principles apply similarly to both products and services. Moreover, it is common for products and services to be offered together, as is the case with restaurants and retail stores. For instance, most flower shops will not only sell you flowers – which are physical products – but can also prepare a bouquet for you – providing an intangible service.

However, the marketing of services can differ from physical product marketing in some important respects. For example, as services lack tangible attributes, they cannot be physically inspected and evaluated prior to purchase. Hence, your service customers will likely depend on your company's supplementary imagery when pre-evaluating your service. This supplementary imagery can include the quality of your advertising, the prestige of your address, and even the design of your letterhead. Prestigious legal firms are famous for employing this kind of supplementary imagery to establish customer trust.

Searching for clues about your service quality, your customers may also be particularly sensitive to your employees' empathy, courtesy, and communication skills. For instance, when you enter a hotel or airplane, the courtesy with which you are greeted may be a good indicator of how comfortable your service experience will be.

By contrast, some teachers and other experts show not courtesy, but arrogance. That is their way of indicating that they hold superior knowledge that cannot be evaluated by a mere novice. However, some seem to enjoy using this tactic so much that they get carried away, attempting to position themselves as having more expertise than they really possess.

To avoid unpleasant surprises, service customers often favor companies that have well-established brand names. For example, some travellers frequent fast-food restaurant chains, because even in an unfamiliar town, the familiar fast-food company logo seems to assure a dependable level of service.

Service and product marketing both require effective positioning. The difference is mainly in how that positioning is accomplished: Service companies typically need to rely more heavily on supplementary imagery to compensate for the intangibility of their offering.

Chapter 5

Leverage Your Brand Equity

Customers instinctively prefer products that are clearly positioned within an organized brand hierarchy. They want to know what makes each brand special.[9] And they don't want to waste their effort trying to sort out a confusing product line. Gunther has taken care of this, ensuring that the LibertyOne and the FriendShip are positioned distinctively with respect to each other.

While the members of a product line need to be distinctive, the brand names on *different* levels of your hierarchy need to *complement* each other. For example, the LibertyOne's full name, the Galactic SpaceJet LibertyOne, is drawn from three levels in the brand hierarchy. Each name has associations that are mutually supportive, and consistent with the product itself:

Brand Name	Association
Galactic	Precision German engineering
SpaceJet	High quality recreational spacecraft
LibertyOne	Youthful independence and adventure

If these associations were not mutually supportive and complementary, they would conflict, weakening the credibility of the brand. For example, if Gunther launched a new spaceship called Galactic SpaceJet *Yogurt*, the high-tech engineering associations of the company and family brand names would be incongruous with the dairy-related nature of the product brand name. Customers would be confused about the meaning of the brand. And dealers, doubting its viability, would be reluctant to carry it. That is why the different levels in your brand hierarchy should be relevant and complementary. (On the other hand, sometimes a completely incongruous name such as Amazon.com can stick, precisely because it is so incongruous. Of course, it helps to have a very substantial advertising budget.)

Take a moment now to review your own brand hierarchy, and the associations you have written beside each brand name. Do the brand names on the different levels seem to complement each other? And within your product lines, are your brands distinctive? If not, then your customers might be feeling confused about the positioning of your products.

Benefit from Your Brand Equity

An important benefit of higher-level brand names is that their associations apply to all the brand names below them. For example, Gunther's SpaceJet, LibertyOne and FriendShip brand names share the precision German engineering associations of his Galactic company brand name. In the same way, your own lower-level brand names will normally share the associations of whatever brand names are above them in your brand hierarchy.

Gunther plans to take advantage of these shared associations when he launches his new two-seater spacecraft, the Galactic SpaceJet *Duet*. Consumers will accept the new Duet product more readily, because it is a member of the trusted Galactic and SpaceJet brand families. By leveraging this brand equity, the Duet should enjoy a significant head start, despite its limited marketing budget. However, if the Duet fails, it could damage the credibility of the Galactic and SpaceJet **parent brands**.

> A brand name that represents an entire product line is known as a **parent brand**. Brands within a product line are known as sub-brands, child brands, or product brands.

Extend Your Product Line

Gunther's SpaceJet Duet is an example of a brand extension. A **brand extension** is a new product that is launched under an already-established brand name. Using an existing brand name can enable you to launch your new product more cost-effectively, by avoiding the expense of establishing an entirely new brand.

There are two kinds of brand extensions: A line extension, and a category extension[10]. A **line extension** is a new member of an *existing* product line. For example, Diet Pepsi® is a line extension of the Pepsi® product line.

For another example, consider a hypothetical bakery owner named Kevin, who sells his "Crunchy" brand of cookies to grocery stores. He is planning to launch a new cookie variety, "Kevin's Crunchy *Pecan* Cookies". As this new pecan cookie is similar to the other cookie flavors in his line, and it shares the "Crunchy" family brand name, it should be considered a *line* extension.

If instead he was planning to launch a new chocolate chip muffin, having never sold muffins before, he would be entering a new *category*. Suppose he calls this new product, "Kevin's Insanely Delicious Chocolate Chip Muffins". Notice that a new family brand, "Insanely Delicious", has been substituted in place of the "Crunchy" *family* brand. But the "Kevin's" *company* brand name is still present. By using an existing brand name – "Kevin's" – to enter a new category (muffins), he is launching not a line extension, but a **category extension**. Both his cookie *line* extension and his muffin *category* extension would benefit from the equity of his established brand names.

Is there room for a line extension in your own brand hierarchy? Any planned line extension should satisfy a substantial need that is not being adequately served by your existing products, or by your competitors' products.

Try adding a line extension to your brand hierarchy drawing now. Near your new line extension brand name, write a list of the most important associations you would like it to have.

By its very nature, a line extension should be similar to the rest of its product line. But your customers need to be able to distinguish it from its product-line peers. Therefore, be sure its associations highlight not only its membership in the brand family, but also the points of difference that make it special.

A line extension can enhance the appeal of your product line. But it may also entail some trade-offs. Let's look at some of the pros and cons.

Line Extension Advantages

The launch of Kevin's new pecan cookies will increase the *variety* offered by his Crunchy cookie line. This should make his cookie line more interesting for his customers. As well, his additional cookie flavor will allow the Crunchy line to occupy more retail shelf space, increasing its *visibility*. This should help draw more attention to his cookies.

Like the members of a human family that help each other, the individual members of a product line can reinforce each other's positioning. For example, Kevin's new pecan-flavored cookie will sell better as a member of the Crunchy product line than it would as an entirely separate product. Thanks to the Crunchy brand's established reputation, Crunchy cookie enthusiasts will have high expectations for the new pecan flavor, and will be eager to try it. Anticipating this consumer enthusiasm, distributors and retailers will be more willing to stock the new flavor. In turn, customers who enjoy the new pecan flavor itself will think more highly of the entire Crunchy product line. Hence, the strength of the individual brands will be mutually reinforcing, allowing greater family brand strength than could be achieved with fewer flavors.

Avoid Confusion & Cannibalization

How many flavors should Kevin have in his cookie line? If he has just one or two flavors, then distributors and retailers may simply ignore his line. They may instead prefer other more complete cookie lines that offer greater sales potential. In this scenario, the addition of several new line extensions could make his product line more attractive for his intermediaries.

However, if numerous additional line extensions are launched, the positioning of Kevin's various cookie varieties might start to overlap. In most cases, this would be undesirable. Overlapped positioning could blur the distinctiveness of the individual cookie products, and confuse customers. Moreover, the overlapped brands would likely **cannibalize** each other's sales. In other words, increased sales of one flavor would reduce the sales of any other similar flavors. And so, Kevin's brands would be fighting against each other, wasting his marketing effort. Therefore, Kevin should recognize that if several different cookie varieties are satisfying the same demand, then one cookie flavor alone may be able to do the job more cost-effectively, with less customer confusion.

With the lure of greater profits, it can be tempting to launch numerous line extensions. By expanding your product line, you may hope to occupy more retail shelf space. Or perhaps you could make better use of your idle production capacity. Or maybe you could allow your sales reps to be more efficient by selling more products on each sales call. These can all be effective ways to increase your profits.

Too Much Choice Can Confuse Customers

On the other hand, if some of the brands in your product line are weak, or if their positioning is not distinctive, you may achieve more by pruning your line, instead of launching new extensions. This is called **brand rationalization**. If you choose to discontinue any brands, plan carefully to offer your existing customers attractive alternative products to which they can migrate. By rationalizing overlapping brands, you may be able to:

- Increase your product line's credibility among your intermediaries
- Reduce customer confusion
- Reduce your overall brand marketing costs.

Nonetheless, a well-positioned line extension can be an effective and economical way to build your business.

To be considered a good line extension candidate, your new product should be similar enough to your existing product line that it will seem to be a natural member of it. But it also needs distinctive characteristics that will help customers distinguish it from its product-line peers. In addition, a line extension will need to generate enough additional sales to justify the expense of launching and maintaining it.

On the other hand, if you wish to launch a new product that does not fit naturally within an existing line, then consider launching your product as a *category extension* instead.

The Ins and Outs of Entering a New Category

As you know, a brand extension can be either a line extension or a category extension. The advantage of a **category extension** is that you can launch a new product *category* that benefits from the associations of your established *company* brand name. For this reason, a category extension can be launched more economically than an entirely separate brand. Let's consider an example.

Gunther is mulling over a possible category extension: A line of radio receivers, named TuneIn, capable of receiving radio broadcasts originating from distant galaxies. But will these radios benefit from his present brand associations? One present brand association is space travel, which could be relevant to cosmic radio technology. As well, the company's association with precision engineering would probably confer upon the radios a high-quality image.

You might be wondering why the TuneIn radios should be considered a category extension, not a line extension. The reason is that these radios are substantially different from the existing SpaceJet spaceship line. Their technology differs, and their markets differ. It follows logically then that they should have a separate family brand name: TuneIn. Yet they would still be marketed under the Galactic company brand name. Hence, they would be referred to as a *category* extension.

Parent Brand Power

Generally, category extensions pose a different kind of challenge than line extensions do. The challenge with a *line* extension is to position it distinctively within its product line. With a *category* extension, by contrast, establishing distinctiveness within a brand family is not the main challenge. Normally, a new product is launched as a *category* extension precisely because it is inherently different, and it cannot fit into an existing product line. So the challenge is to somehow link the category extension to the company brand, so as to benefit from the parent brand's reputation. And so it is the similarities that a category extension shares with its parent brand that should be emphasized.

For example, Honda's line of electric generators started out as a category extension from the company's motorcycles. What do generators and motorcycles have in common? Engine technology. And it is this shared technology that stands out in customers' minds. Many years later, these generators still benefit from the parent brand equity.

Kevin's new muffin category extension is another example. His muffins are baked goods, which is just what his company is famous for. Provided that he emphasizes how his muffins are consistent with the "Kevin's" company brand reputation, his muffin category extension will benefit.

Avoid Blurring Your Brand Image

Why, then, do some leading consumer products companies avoid prominently linking their product brands with their company brand names? Consider companies like Procter & Gamble and Unilever, that sell products as diverse as laundry detergent, facial tissue, and toothpaste. Why do the names of powerful companies like these appear on their packaging only in small, inconspicuous text? Perhaps these firms are concerned that strongly associating their products with their parent brand would indirectly link their individual products with each other. This could blur their respective products' positioning. For instance, Tide® laundry detergent would not benefit from the dental hygiene associations of Crest® toothpaste, as these two products serve entirely different purposes.

But does it not cost a great deal more to establish such brands as independent entities? Normally, yes. An entirely independent brand having no relationship to any parent brand will have to build its own brand equity from scratch. That can be very expensive. However, products like Tide® and Crest® generally have long life spans, and therefore may seem worth the considerable investment needed to establish them as independent brands.

Branding Short-Lived Products

In contrast, some products have life spans that are too short to justify investing in separate brand names. For example, many consumer electronics products survive only briefly before being replaced by the next year's model. And so manufacturers of these products avoid investing in individual product brand names. Instead, they invest more heavily in the *parent* brand name, while using only model numbers to identify the short-lived *individual* products. Sony is a case in point; their *company* name is prominently featured on all of their products, along with the appropriate *family* brand name, such as Handycam®. But the individual products are typically distinguished only by letters and numbers.

Perhaps electronics manufacturers have a further reason to emphasize their *company* brand, without distinguishing their *individual* products with memorable names: While laundry soap and toothpaste tend to be habitual purchases that consumers can make unassisted, electronics products are more complicated and confusing, and some consumers must rely on retail salespeople for guidance. As retailers have significant influence at the crucial moment of purchase, manufacturers may be all the more interested in keeping them happy. One way to do that might be for the manufacturer to give each retail chain a slightly different version of a product. Each version could have a slightly different model number to thwart direct price comparisons by consumers.

Brainstorm a Category Extension

As with a line extension, a well-positioned category extension can reward you with a steady stream of profits for years to come. But to realize that potential, you will first need to identify a suitable category extension candidate. How can you do that? Try using an *opportunity table*, as you have already done in a previous chapter. To see how this works, take a look at the one completed by Carrie O'Kay, a fictitious owner of a fast-food restaurant called O'Kay Cookin'.

To complete her opportunity table, Carrie first wrote a description of her existing business in row #1. Then she scanned the row, looking for ways to improve her business. Noticing only three product lines in the Benefits cell, she decided to add some similar product lines in the second row, including salads, soups, and desserts.

Row	Brand Extension Opportunities	Carrie's Required Resources *Expertise & Assets*	Carrie's Current & Potential Benefits *Products & Reputation*	Carrie's Current and Potential Customers
1	Existing fast food restaurant.	Food-service equipment and know-how, plus knowledge of advertising design, purchasing, and bookkeeping.	• Products: O'Kay burgers, sandwiches, soft drinks. • Associations: Scrumptious food, served quickly and conveniently in pleasant surroundings suitable for casual get-togethers.	Hungry folk passing through, or living within a 10 mile radius.
2	New menu categories.	Additional food preparation know-how.	• O'Kay salads, soups, & desserts. • Associations: Same as above.	Same as above.
3	Catering service.	Additional food preparation and serving know-how. Organization and sales skills.	• Served at customer's location. • A broader menu of food items suitable for catering. • Associations: Delectable food served at customers' choice of location.	Business event organizers, and people throwing private parties.
4	Carrie O'Kay's Karaoke.	Same as Row #1, plus karaoke equipment and additional restaurant space.	Same as Row #1, plus entertainment.	People seeking food and entertainment.

Row	Your Brand Extension Opportunities	Your Required Resources *Expertise & Assets*	The Current & Potential Benefits *Products & Reputation*	Your Current and Potential Customers
1				
2				
3				
4				

Fortunately, the other cells did not need to be changed very much to accommodate her new products.

Scanning the columns again, she realized that she could expand her business not only by adding new physical products, but also by adding a new service. It seemed that a catering service could be easily accommodated by her existing expertise and assets. The greatest impact might be that she would have to use more proactive sales tactics to target a different kind of customer – event organizers and people throwing parties – rather than simply taking orders in her restaurant. Carrie was confident that this category extension would be quite manageable.

However, when considering Row #4, she felt some apprehension about the prospect of having to construct additional restaurant space in order to launch the new venture that would have been called "Carrie O'Kay's Karaoke".

Try completing your own opportunity table now, and see if you can generate some category extension ideas for your business. Let your ideas flow, without being too judgmental. If you would prefer a smooth transition to new areas of business, then you should avoid major changes in too many areas at once. But if you can tolerate more risk and have sufficient financial resources, you can consider launching an entirely unrelated breakthrough product as a separate brand. In any case, add your category extensions or new products to your brand hierarchy diagram.

Next, return to your SWOT matrix, and find a suitable spot in it for your proposed new brand. Does it still make sense in this context? Your proposed brand should help you balance your strengths and weaknesses against your opportunities and threats.

Positioning on a Perceptual Map

It is important to understand how each of your brands is positioned with respect to its competitors. For this purpose, perceptual maps are a handy tool. Try sketching one now for your new brand extension. If you don't have actual market research data, then just use your best estimates.

Does your perceptual map indicate that your new brand is positioned similarly to your rivals' brands? If so, you may be forced to compete head-on with them. This could require greater advertising, promoting, and discounting. The additional marketing effort and expense will sap your energy and your profits. If your competitors value their position in the market, and if they have the necessary human and financial resources to resist you, then you may be faced with a costly and protracted struggle. You may also have difficulty persuading distributors and retailers to carry your product in the first place, if they do not see how it will add meaningful variety to their product selection.

To avoid this problem, you can either target the same customers by offering different benefits, or target different customers altogether. For example, if you are selling candy, you could offer unusual flavors like grass and dandelion. Or you could target pet owners, who might want to feed your candy to their pet porcupines.

Sometimes, an established product needs to be repositioned, as the market evolves over time. In such cases, a perceptual map can be a helpful visual aid, as the following diagram illustrates.

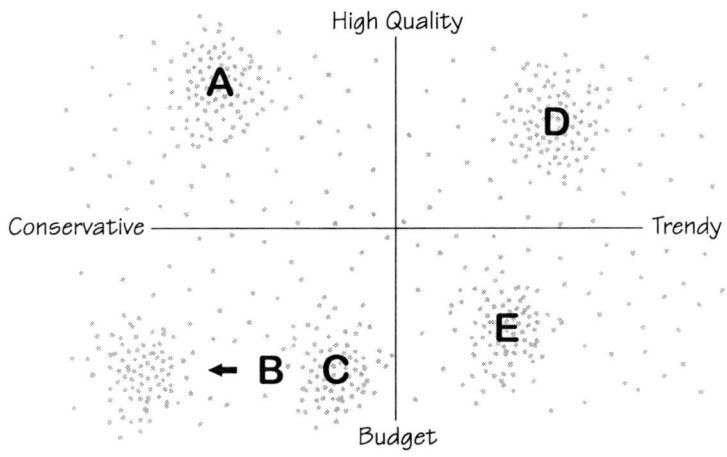

On this perceptual map, brands B and C appear to be too close to each other. Brand B could benefit if it were repositioned to the left, away from Brand C, to satisfy other more conservative customers.

If you want to compare your product with its rivals on more than two dimensions, then instead of using a perceptual map, you can list your products in a grid. In the following grid, the positioning of three hypothetical apparel brands is represented by the letters A, B, and C. The placement of these three letters in the first row indicates that brand A uses natural fabrics, whereas B uses synthetics. The second row indicates that A is the most fashionable, and the third row indicates that C is the most expensive. This kind of grid can enable you to compare brand positioning on more than two dimensions at once. As a visual aid, you can draw colored lines to connect all the As together, all the Bs together, and all the Cs together.

Natural Fabrics	A		C		B	Synthetic
Conservative	C		B	A		Fashionable
Low-Priced		B	A		C	High-Priced

Can They Count on Your Quality?

Consistency builds trust. Hence, consistent quality across your product line will help your brand reputation. Without consistent quality, your customers will be unsure of what your brand stands for.

If you start with a medium quality brand, and try to launch a high-quality extension from it, your customers will be skeptical. On the other hand, if you launch a low-quality extension instead, it will be more believable, but it might also degrade the image of your parent brand. For example, a prestigious piano manufacturer, serving a relatively small market of discerning, sophisticated customers, may wish to target the much larger market for budget pianos. Rather than selling lower-priced pianos under their prestigious flagship brand name, they could sell the lower priced line as an entirely separate brand, produced in offshore factories, without any clear connection to the parent brand. This strategy could allow the company to profit from the large budget-priced piano market, while preserving the exclusivity and prestige of their flagship brand.

In other cases, a company might want to avoid linking a new product with the parent brand for the opposite reason: They might want to avoid tainting the new brand with some inappropriate associations of the parent brand. Perhaps Toyota launched its luxury Lexus® cars as an entirely separate brand for this reason. While the regular Toyota line was highly respected, it was not perceived as a luxury line. Therefore any association with it would blur the Lexus's intended luxury status.

In both of these cases – the pianos and the cars – the new products were launched as entirely separate brands, not as category extensions. This is because the existing flagship piano brand needed its exclusivity preserved. And the new luxury car brand needed its exclusivity to be independently established.

Exclusivity tells customers that a brand is special. It's not just a matter of snob appeal. If a brand is truly special, it must be clearly positioned that way, without compromise. It's a matter of keeping the positioning absolutely straight in customers' minds. And it's a matter of commanding the premium price needed to support the premium quality of the brand.

Why Launch a Brand Extension?

Launching a new brand extension can be strategically advantageous in a number of ways. As you read the following scenarios, consider how a brand extension could benefit your own business.

- Launching a line extension can enable you to occupy more retail shelf space. This can increase the visibility of your product line. Some firms expand their product lines with the sole intention of monopolizing limited shelf space at the expense of their rivals. However, retailers may be skeptical of this kind of

maneuver, unless each product in the line is positioned distinctively, and valued by consumers.
- Customers tend to be attracted to product lines that offer reasonable variety and choice. A line extension may enable you to offer that.
- By launching successive new line extensions, you can gradually build a full suite of complementary products, serving as a complete solution to your customers' needs. For example, while word-processing software by itself is useful, it is even more useful when combined with spreadsheet and e-mail programs, as is the case with Microsoft Office®.
- Brand extensions can help you achieve a cost advantage through economies of scale or scope. For example, by adding extensions to his cookie line, Kevin the baker can spread his fixed costs – such as his rent – over a larger number of cookies. This can allow him to price his cookies lower than the cookies of other bakeries that operate at a lower volume.
- Do you have idle production capacity? If so, you may be able to make use of it by launching appropriate brand extensions. For example, if your restaurant is normally open only for lunch and supper, you can introduce a line of breakfast meals, so that your cooking and dining facilities will no longer be idle in the early morning hours.
- It's normally cheaper to introduce a brand extension than to launch an entirely separate brand. That's because a brand extension can benefit from its parent brand's reputation. By contrast, to launch an entirely separate brand, you'll need to build its reputation from scratch – and that costs money.
- A low-priced brand extension can serve as an entry-level product for first-time customers. The aim would be to earn their lifetime loyalty, so that they would

eventually trade up to your higher-priced models. Some software companies introduce bare-bones versions of their products free of charge or at a very low price, hoping that customers will learn to like the software enough to eventually upgrade, and pay for the full-featured version. For this upgrade strategy to be successful, you must maintain consistent quality across your product line, even at different price points, in order to earn your customers' trust.
- A flagship brand extension can add to the status and the credibility of your company's products. For example, after seeing a famous musician perform on a deluxe guitar model in concert, amateur musicians may be sufficiently impressed to purchase even the standard models that are more affordable for them.
- Brand extensions can inspire employees and generate goodwill. For example, to generate goodwill, a symphony orchestra can launch a free children's concert series as a brand extension, in addition to its regular concerts. Or a sports organization could launch a series of events for disabled people.
- Some brand extensions are launched just for the fun of it, to indulge the passions and personal interests of the business owner. For example, some software products are developed for personal reasons, and yet they still achieve popularity among customers. And some popular musicians produce brand extensions in the form of new albums, which they create for their own satisfaction, as well as to appeal to their fans.

Chapter 6

Be in the Right Place at the Right Time

The prospect of a new product launch can be exciting. But before you take the plunge, consider how the timing of your launch might impact your chances for success. If your product category is in the introductory or growth stage of its product life cycle (PLC), your chances for success will be greater. In contrast, the maturity or decline stages of the PLC tend to be more challenging, especially if you are just entering the market.

How a Product Life Cycle Starts

Product life cycles can follow a variety of different patterns. But they all tend to start out the same way: An innovative technology is invented or a trend-setting new product is launched. This draws the attention of rival firms to the existence of a previously unrecognized market or segment. Typically, some of these rival firms will then scramble to enter the market, each offering their own solution to the newly-recognized customer need. As more and more potential customers become aware of the new product category and its benefits, demand increases. As long as demand keeps increasing, firms in the market will typically be able to survive and prosper by attracting first-time customers. The firms that increase their sales at a rate faster than the market growth rate will gradually capture a larger market share. On the other hand, any firms that grow more slowly than the market growth rate will gradually lose share.

> **Primary demand** is the entire demand for a product category – such as frozen pizza – including demand for all competing brands. Primary demand increases during the growth stage of the product life cycle (PLC). As growth in primary demand slows or stops altogether, any firms wishing to grow will typically try to increase *selective* demand for their own products, at the expense of their rivals' market share. **Selective demand** – or **secondary demand** – is the demand for specific brands within a category.

Industry Consolidation

Eventually, market growth will slow down, as the supply of new customers is depleted. This is an unpleasant turn of events for companies that are accustomed to rapid growth. With the stagnation of growth in **primary demand**, some firms may attempt to expand their sales by increasing **selective demand** for their own products, at the expense of their rivals.

As battles for market share erupt, prices may be cut. This erodes profits, and consequently, the weaker players in the market start to flounder. The industry undergoes a **consolidation** or "shakeout" stage, where some companies withdraw from the market, some go out of business, and other firms are bought out by their larger rivals. The winners will be those with a special advantage, such as

Growth and Market Share

having the lowest costs, or the most effectively positioned products, or the strongest customer relationships.

Competition in the Maturity Stage

The maturity stage of the PLC starts when the market stops growing and demand stabilizes. If there are just a handful of dominant firms remaining, each firm may realize that its rivals cannot be defeated, and that price wars will only destroy profits. Prices may remain stable.

However, if the total industry production capacity greatly exceeds demand, then even large firms may be motivated to cut prices in an attempt to cover their fixed costs and maintain their break-even sales volume.

On the other hand, if the remaining firms are numerous and small, none will be large enough to effectively punish price-cutting. In this case, price competition is likely to be more intense, as the more aggressive firms discount their prices to gain market share.

Another characteristic of the maturity stage may be increasing product **commoditization**. This occurs if competing firms imitate each other's successful products. As previously differentiated products gradually become more like undifferentiated commodities, some firms may resort to competing on price. If product commoditization increases price competition in this manner, then the firm with the lowest costs will have an advantage. Alternatively, some firms may be able to escape price competition by positioning their brands distinctively, even if they are physically and functionally similar to their competitors.

In other situations, demand can become more fragmented. As customers become increasingly familiar with the product category, they may start wanting special features to satisfy their particular needs. Or as they become more sophisticated, some customers of complex products may no longer require much product education and personal service. They may instead prefer competitive pricing and convenience.[11] For example, they may choose to purchase computers economically over the Internet, rather than from local high-service shops. Or they may prefer to purchase stocks and investments from low-commission self-serve websites, rather than through full-service stock brokers. Firms can profit by recognizing and satisfying these needs as they emerge.

Prospering in the Maturity Stage

Across different product categories, the maturity stage of the product life cycle can vary in length, continuing for weeks, months, years, or even centuries. Every PLC is unique. Profitability can vary as well. For example, a long maturity stage can be very profitable for dominant brands in stable industries – such as household consumer products like laundry detergent. In contrast, industries beset by excess fixed production capacity tend to be more prone to price competition and much less profitable during their maturity stage.

Sometimes, a PLC can be unexpectedly disrupted in its maturity stage. Demand can rise or fall sharply, due to demographic shifts, new technologies, or government deregulation. These disruptions can offer opportunities for new growth, for firms that are ready to satisfy whatever new customer needs emerge. In recent decades, for example, the maturity stage of the telephone industry has been disrupted by government deregulation, as well as new technologies such as cell phones, e-mail, and Internet phone services. Some of these new technologies have proved to be wildly successful offshoots from the main telephone PLC.

In some industries – such as automobile manufacturing – **cyclical demand fluctuations** can repeatedly occur during the maturity stage of the PLC. The impact of periodic decreases in demand can be exacerbated by inflexible production capacity. For example, some automobile manufacturers have large production plants that cannot be easily disposed of, and must be kept running in order to cover their fixed costs. If the demand for new vehicles slows down, then these firms tend to compete vigorously for market share.

> When the economy slows down, people tend to restrict their spending to the purchase of essential items. They make fewer discretionary purchases, such as vacation trips. And so the demand for products like these can fluctuate, increasing and decreasing concurrently with cycles in the economy. We can refer to these changes in demand as **cyclical demand fluctuations**.

How can you increase sales and profitability during the maturity stage of your PLC? One way is to increase your sales volume by launching new brand extensions. Or you can build customer trust in your brand by improving your product quality. Or else you can encourage *existing* customers to use your products more often, or on different occasions. For example, on the insides of breakfast cereal cartons, you'll often find recipes that include the cereal as an ingredient. This encourages consumers to use more of the breakfast cereal product. Online retailers employ a different tactic for the same purpose: They regularly email their existing customers to keep them informed about new merchandise and special offers. This can increase profits by encouraging more business from existing customers.

Can You Earn Profits in the Decline Stage?

If a product category starts to lose popularity among consumers, its life cycle will enter the decline stage. Why does this happen? Possibly because new products or technologies start replacing the old, much as cell-phones have reduced the need for phone booths. Sometimes, products just go out of fashion, as hula-hoops and platform shoes did. Demographic shifts can also spell the end of a PLC, as customers grow older, for example. This is the case with the market for the popular songs of bygone decades. These songs are heard less often as their fans grow old and pass away.

The decline stage of a PLC can be rapid or gradual. For example, analog music audiocassettes declined rapidly as higher quality music CDs replaced them, whereas cigarettes have declined much more slowly, as customers have gradually recognized the health risks.

What will happen to your firm if your product life cycle starts to decline? You and your rivals may be reluctant to exit the market if you have made large investments in technology, intellectual property, or production facilities that cannot be sold or easily converted to other uses. As the market shrinks, you may be caught in a struggle to maintain your respective sales levels, at each others' expense. Price wars can break out, and profits may plummet. However, if enough firms are forced out of the market through bankruptcy, or if they exit by choice, you may be able to raise your prices and return to profitability, as long as there is sufficient residual demand.

Chapter 7

What is Your Profit Potential?

Whatever your stage in the product life cycle, you will need to satisfy your customers. One way to satisfy customers is to offer good value for their money. But how will your customers judge the value of your product?

Your customers will evaluate your product according to how well it seems able to satisfy their needs. They will also compare it with its alternatives. They will compare its quality, features, and price, with emphasis on their own preferences. For example, when comparing two sets of tools in a hardware store, you might prefer the more expensive one because it has more tools, or it comes with a handy carrying case. Despite these advantages, a friend of yours might prefer the cheaper tool set because he is more interested in saving his money.

Thus, the purchase decisions of both you and your friend are determined by your respective perceptions and preferences. And so the idea of getting good value for your money can have very different meanings for different people. A bargain for one person may be a waste of money for another.

What Is The Right Price For Your Product?

If each customer values your new product according to his or her own personal criteria, how can you determine what price to charge? No matter what price you charge, you won't likely please everyone. But you can minimize the range of opinions among your customers by targeting a particular segment. If the customers in your target segment share the same needs, attitudes, and income levels, for example, they will more likely value your product consistently.

A market research firm can help you set the price for your new product. But if you can't afford to hire a market research firm, you can simply ask your customers for their opinions. Show your product and its leading competitors to at least 20 knowledgeable customers from your target segment. Ask them to guess the actual product prices. This will tell you how they value your product relative to its competitors.

Keep in mind that in the actual marketplace, some competing products may be priced too high and may be losing market share as a result. Or else they may be increasing their market share by charging low prices, or by advertising heavily. Other products may fetch higher prices because they are sold in convenient or prestigious retail outlets. Considering these factors, you will need to involve some personal judgment in your pricing decisions.

What about changing the price of an existing product? If you think your price may be too high, you could try putting it on sale for a while, and see if your sales volume increases enough to more than compensate for your lost margin. However, this kind of experiment can mislead you. That's because customers may be more interested in a product if it's "on sale" at $10 – because it seems like a bargain – than if it's regularly priced at $10. Moreover, by lowering your price even temporarily, you may devalue your product in your customers' minds. Or after your promotional sale, they may postpone further purchases, believing that you will eventually put your product "on sale" again. Given these potential pitfalls, even basic market research will prove a safer way to evaluate pricing alternatives than experimenting with your actual prices.

Once you have settled on a new price, you will want to make the change without upsetting your customers. For packaged goods, one way to increase your percentage margins involves lowering your price by a small amount while you decrease your package size by a greater amount. For instance, a 0.5 kg box of breakfast cereal priced at $10 ($20/kg) can become a 0.4 kg box priced at $9 ($22.50/kg). Alternatively, you can hold your price steady while decreasing your package size, though the resulting loss of value will be more obvious to your customers. To raise your price, you can temporarily bundle your product with a free offer: For example, you can offer a free soft-drink when customers purchase a pizza at your new higher price. Later, discontinue the free soft-drink offer, but keep your pizza price at the new higher level.

Are Your Product Usage Costs Too High?

Naturally, customers are attracted to reasonably-priced products. But the full cost of some products includes much more than the purchase price alone. The full cost – or **life cycle cost** – may include the cost of usage, maintenance, repair, and disposal. And so, if your product does not perform well over the long haul, and ends up costing a great deal to own, your customers could become dissatisfied, even if they were pleased with the initial purchase price. For instance, if you manufacture an electric drill that breaks down frequently, then the cost and inconvenience of having to repair it will disappoint your customers.

> The entire cost of purchasing, maintaining, and disposing of a durable product, is known as its **life cycle cost**. Here, the word *life cycle* refers to the span of a product's useful life. It does not refer to the change in demand for your product category over time, known as your **product life cycle**.

Your customers may not pay much heed to life cycle costs when purchasing your product. Instead, they will tend to be more focussed on their initial perceptions of it, and their immediate cash outlay. But if your product's life cycle costs later turn out to be disappointingly high, then your customers will experience dissatisfaction.

The Danger of Dissatisfaction

Dissatisfied customers tend to feel angry and frustrated, and they may seek an outlet for their negative emotions. If your product does not perform as expected, they may feel that a bond of trust has been broken. Consequently, they may feel that complaining to your company would be pointless, as your firm cannot be trusted anyway. To vent their anger and frustration, they may instead criticize your product to friends, relatives, neighbors, and on Internet forums. To other potential customers, their negative remarks may seem more credible than your advertising. If, as a result, a great many potential customers are persuaded not to purchase your product, your most determined marketing efforts may be defeated.

Don't Betray Your Customers

"It's a nice quiet neighborhood. There's a small airport nearby, but it's not very busy. This is a great place to retire!"

"Okay, we'll buy this house!"

A short while later, a new town council is elected. They forget that even communities need dependable benefits and consistent positioning ...

"If we let the new flight school operate 25 planes and 17 helicopters, the airport will earn $10,000. We need to prove that the airport can make a profit."

But there are thousands of retired people living nearby. They pay millions in property taxes. They thought we had a quiet little airport. They won't like having a lot more noise.

That's their problem. If they don't like it, they can move elsewhere.

"What a racket! This turned out to be a lousy place to retire!"

"Let's move some place where we'll be treated better. We'll take our $10 million retirement savings with us."

Segmentation and Positioning for Satisfaction

How can you avoid customer dissatisfaction? One way is to sell your product only to those customers who are likely to be satisfied with it. This requires effective segmentation, targeting, and positioning. You should target only appropriate segments. And your positioning should be consistent with the benefits your product actually offers, so that your customers will understand the true nature of your product before they purchase it.

If you sell your product to inappropriate customers, chances are they will be unhappy with it. For example, if you produce an action-adventure movie, but position it as a sophisticated comedy-romance, you will attract the wrong audience, and they will likely be disappointed. Or if you position your town as an attractive place for affluent people to retire, and then ruin their quality of life with excessive aircraft noise, they too will be disappointed. They may voice their disappointment to their friends elsewhere, and the reputation of your town will suffer.

Listen to Customer Complaints

To find out whether your product is satisfying your customers, carefully track and document all customer feedback, including complaints. Analysis of this data will help you detect patterns and trends in your customers' concerns.

Train your employees to listen empathetically to customer complaints, and empower them to solve problems expeditiously. Not only will this help defuse any customer anger, but it will likely earn significant customer gratitude and goodwill as well.

By listening to customer complaints, you can learn how to improve your product quality. Higher product quality can help you minimize customer disappointment, product returns, and warranty claims – while improving your reputation.

How Product Quality Can Impact Your Profits

One way to attract new customers is to offer high quality goods. This can lead to increased sales and profits. But high quality can also help you retain your *existing* customers, and this is very important.

Why is customer retention important? Because the effort needed to retain existing customers is typically much less than the effort needed to attract new ones. In fact, you may need several transactions just to break even on the cost of attracting each new customer. In other words, each time a customer defects before you have broken-even on the cost of attracting them, your bottom-line profit will be negatively impacted. On the other hand, the customers that you do retain may have a substantial **lifetime value** that repays your marketing efforts many times over.

> **Customer lifetime value** refers to the total profits (discounted to the present) that you can expect to earn by satisfying a customer's needs with your products throughout his or her entire life.

As an added bonus, by satisfying your *existing* customers, you may be able to actually increase your sales to them. This can be a very cost-effective way to grow. For example, imagine that you sell bottled drinks in a mature market where few new customers can be found. You could try to increase your share of your existing customers' beverage consumption. If a customer normally spends $10 a day on their total beverage purchases, you could try to increase your share from 20% of that amount to 30%. This would further increase your customers' lifetime value to your firm, perhaps without significantly increasing your marketing costs.

> To satisfy a particular need, your *existing* customers can purchase either your product, or its competitors in the same category. If 20% of your existing customers' need is satisfied by *your* product, then your **customer share** is 20% – even if you have only one customer. Customer share is also known as **share of wallet**, or in the case of food, *share of stomach*.

Satisfying your customers with high product quality, superior service, and effective complaint resolution, can have an enormous positive impact on your customer retention rate, and on the profitability of your firm.

How Profits Are Earned

The price you set for your product will influence your profits in two ways:
- Higher prices may reduce your sales *volume*, if your customers are price-sensitive.
- At the same time, higher prices will increase your profit *margin* on each sale.

Profits are earned one sale at a time, by charging a price that is higher than your product's variable cost. This variable cost includes the cost of the product itself, known as its **cost of goods sold (CGS)**. The variable cost also includes any other costs – such as sales commissions – that vary directly with sales of your product. The difference between your product's selling price and its variable cost is its **contribution margin per unit**. Each time you sell your product, the unit contribution margin you earn adds to your **total contribution margin** or **total margin dollars**. Your total margin dollars must be sufficient to pay for your product's fixed **marketing expenses**. These fixed expenses can include advertising, marketing research, and slotting allowances.

Total Margin Dollars and Net Contribution

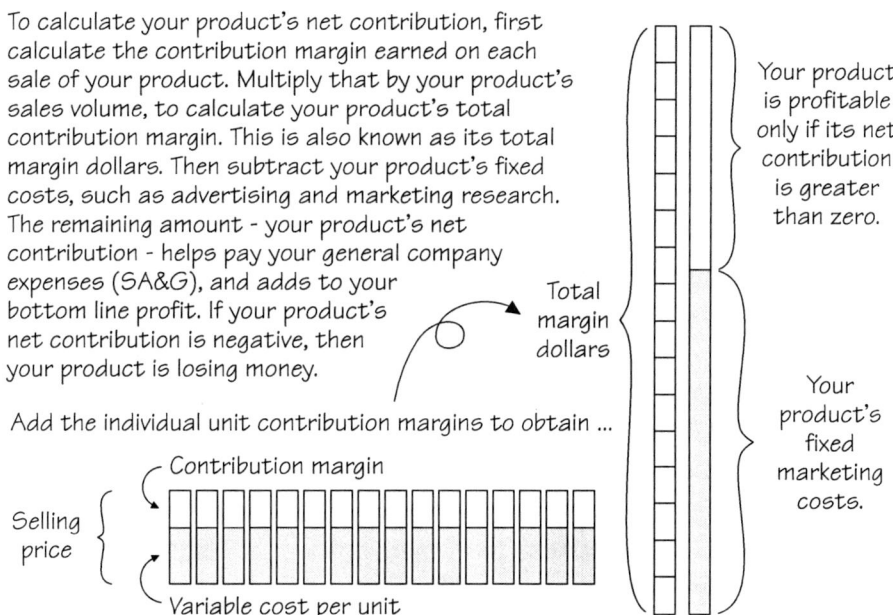

If your total margin dollars are not sufficient to cover your brand's fixed marketing expenses, then your brand is not profitable. This is normal when you are first launching your brand, and you are promoting heavily to attract new customers. But in the long run, your total margin dollars must exceed your product's fixed marketing costs. Whatever is left over is your brand's **net contribution**.

Your brand's net contribution helps cover your firm's **general and administrative costs** (or **G&A expenses**, or SA&G), such as your lease payments and office personnel costs. Whatever amount is left over will add to your bottom line profit.

> In producing and marketing your product, you may incur **fixed costs** that do not vary directly with sales volume. Your product's direct fixed costs can include marketing research and slotting fees. Other *indirect* fixed costs (SA&G) can include rent and utilities. In contrast, **variable costs** are those that do vary according to your production or sales volume. Sales commissions are an example. While this is a simplification of a complex topic, understanding the basic distinction between fixed and variable costs can help you make sound business decisions.

How Price Sensitivity Can Impact Profits

Is there any way to tell in advance whether a new product will be profitable? Fortunately, there are some simple calculations you can perform, before your product is launched. Let's return to the story of our baker friend, Kevin, to see how these calculations work.

When Kevin was considering launching his Insanely Delicious muffin line, one of his first concerns was how price-sensitive his customers would be. In other words, would his customers buy a great many more muffins if he sold them at a lower price? After testing his muffins at different price points in half a dozen grocery stores, Kevin determined that his customers were indeed quite price-sensitive. In other words, a lower muffin price did result in a higher muffin sales volume.

Kevin's market test results illustrate how price can influence sales volume. The way in which your customers change their purchasing behavior in reaction to your price is known as their **price sensitivity**.

There are a number of factors that can influence the price sensitivity of your customers. Your customers will tend to be more price-sensitive if they have easy access to other attractively-priced alternatives. They will also be more price-sensitive if they consider the purchase amount of your product to be a significant portion of their budget. Even a high-priced muffin can seem unaffordable if they think of it as a part of their annual family food bill. These are the circumstances in Kevin's muffin market, as consumers could easily switch to competing muffins on adjacent store shelves, and would readily do so in an effort to control their annual household food expenses.

In this price-sensitive market, Kevin could lose a significant portion of his sales if he fails to quickly match any special discount deals offered by his rivals. On the other hand, by consistently matching or beating their discounts, Kevin may be able to teach his rivals that competing on price will be futile.

Pricing for Maximum Profit

Using his market test results, Kevin calculates that at a wholesale price of one dollar per muffin, he would sell 1000 muffins per day. (The grocery retailers would pay $1, and would then mark up his muffins to $1.25 each, to earn a 20% margin. That is, $0.25/$1.25 = 20%.) At this volume, Kevin's muffins would cost $0.60 each to make and sell. His contribution margin per muffin would be $1 − $0.60 = $0.40 per muffin. His total margin dollars would be 1000 muffins x $0.40 profit per muffin = $400 total margin dollars per day.

How Price Affects Unit Margins

At a wholesale price of $1, the unit contribution margin is $0.40, but not many muffins sell.

At the lower $0.80 price, the unit contribution margin is smaller, but more muffins sell. On the other hand, at this higher production volume, the cost is somewhat lower, which increases the contribution margin by 5 cents.

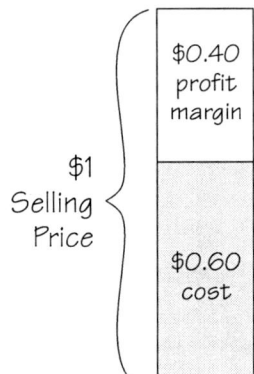
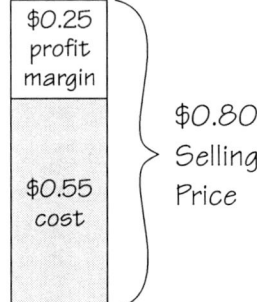

Alternatively, if he matches his rivals' wholesale price of $0.80 each, more consumers will switch to his muffins, preferring their superior taste. (Retailers will mark up his muffins to $1 each.) In this case, he will sell 2000 muffins per day. Since he would be baking them in larger batches, his variable costs would be a tad lower, at $0.55 each. This would leave a unit contribution margin of $0.25. Though the unit margin would be smaller, his total margin dollars would be greater, at 2000 muffins x $0.25 = $500 per day.

At first, Kevin is not sure whether to set his wholesale price at one dollar per muffin, or at $0.80 per muffin. At $0.80 per muffin, he expects his rivals will initially resist his product introduction by cutting their prices, which would slow his market penetration.

However, his cookie line is highly profitable, and could subsidize his muffins during a lengthy period of rival price discounting. And if he can sell 2000 muffins per day, he will achieve the lowest costs in the local muffin industry. This will enable him to beat his rivals' prices if he chooses to. With this reasoning in mind, he musters the confidence to settle on a wholesale price of $0.80 per muffin.

How Price Affects Total Margin Dollars

How to Analyze Pricing Scenarios

The following table shows how Kevin calculates his total margin dollars at two different muffin prices.

Line	Kevin's Muffins	Price 1	Price 2
1	Wholesale price	$1	$0.80
2	Estimated unit sales volume	1000	2000
3	Estimated variable costs per unit	$0.60	$0.55
4	Estimated contribution margin per unit (Line 1 – Line 3)	$0.40	$0.25
5	Total margin dollars (Line 2 x Line 4)	$400	$500

To perform the same calculations for your own new product, complete the following table. If you do not have actual market test data, then just use your best estimates.

Line	Your Product	Price 1	Price 2
1	Selling price		
2	Estimated sales volume in units		
3	Estimated production cost per unit		
4	Estimated profit margin per unit (Line 1 – Line 3)		
5	Total margin dollars (Line 2 x Line 4)		

Enter two different feasible prices for your product. Your price is the amount you receive, whether wholesale or retail. Next, enter the quantity you believe you could sell at each price. The more you sell, the lower your production cost may be. Estimate your variable cost at each different price point. Then, calculate your contribution margin. To do this, subtract your variable cost from your selling price. Next, multiply your unit contribution margin by your sales volume to calculate your total margin dollars. For additional pricing scenarios, add additional columns on the right side of the table.

The above table should help you estimate which price will yield the greatest total margin dollars. How might your rivals react to this price? If they try to block your entry with discounting, how long could you survive? Is your product positioned distinctively and attractively enough that your customers would buy it, regardless of rival price-discounting?

When do Customers Prefer High Prices?

When setting your price, keep in mind that the relationship between price and demand can differ from one product to another. In most cases, price and demand are inversely related. That is, the lower the price, the greater the demand. For example, your local grocer will probably sell more oranges this week if he cuts the price by ten percent, all else being equal.

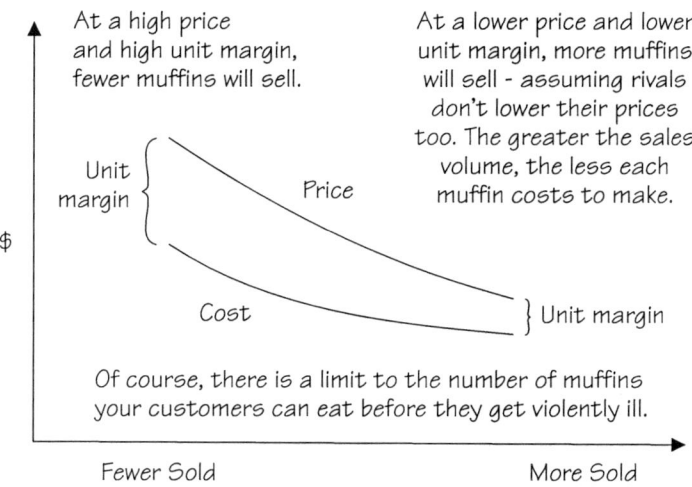

In other cases, however, a low price can undermine consumer confidence in a product's quality or prestige. This is especially true with products that are difficult to evaluate. For example, an anti-wrinkle skin cream may need a high price, or its target customers will not believe how rare and mysteriously potent its ingredients are. And without a high price, some brand-name perfumes would lack sufficient prestige for their target customers. By contrast, products that are essential, and have no substitutes – such as some pharmaceutical items – may sell at a steady pace, regardless of their price, as long as they remain affordable.

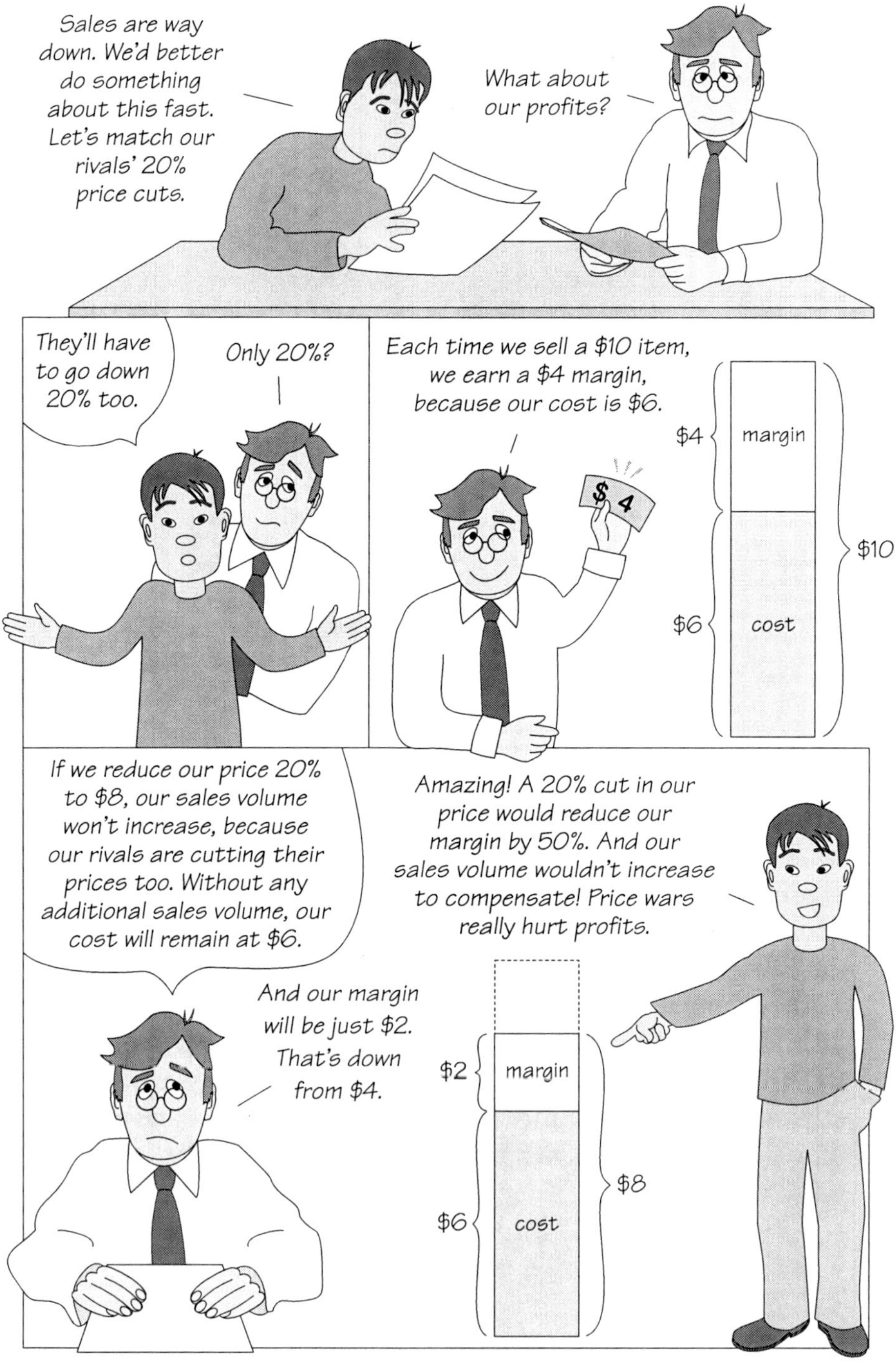

These examples illustrate how consumers can perceive the relationship between price and value in different ways, and how that can impact your sales volume.

How Will Your Rivals React?

Your rivals might respond to your new product introduction with aggressive discounting and coupons, or with increased advertising. These tactics can distract your potential customers, causing them to overlook your product. If, as a result, your product fails to generate sales, it could lose credibility with your salespeople and distribution channels.

To stay in the game, you may need to respond with your own discounts or other promotions. Your competitors may discount their prices not only to retain their market share, but also to discourage you, and persuade you to abandon the market. Try to be financially and mentally prepared for this kind of psychological warfare.

On the other hand, if your rivals believe that you are exceptionally committed or well-financed, they may not bother trying to discourage you at all. For example, if they are aware that you have made large, irreversible investments in production equipment, retail locations, or research and development, they may conclude that you will not be easily discouraged.

The Trouble with Fixed Costs

Your product-related marketing costs will normally be of two types: variable and fixed. Your variable costs are the ones that increase as you sell more of your product. Sales commissions are an example of variable marketing costs. In contrast, fixed costs remain the same, regardless of sales volume. Kevin's fixed marketing costs include the cost of his monthly newspaper advertising contract and his slotting allowances.

Fixed costs pose a special problem, because they exist even if your sales volume is zero. To pay your fixed costs, you will need to maintain a certain minimum volume of sales. But if there are not enough customers in your target segment to achieve that minimum volume of sales, then your product will never be profitable. Therefore, before you enter a market segment, be sure that it is large enough for you to cover your fixed costs.

Is Your Segment Large Enough?

How large should your segment be? To answer that question, let's consider Kevin's situation. From his market tests, Kevin calculates that, based on a total market demand of 5000 muffins per day, his 40% share will earn a daily net contribution of $300. By this estimate, his muffin market is large enough to be worth serving, because it will generate a positive net contribution.

Take a look at the diagram to see how he made that calculation. Then calculate the total margin dollar figure for your own product in the same way. Would your total margin dollar amount be large enough to cover your product's own marketing costs? If so, would the remaining net contribution be sufficient to justify your effort?

Could Your Segment Shrink?

Market segments tend to change. A market segment that is large enough today might be in the process of shrinking. It might eventually become too small to be profitable. For example, if you are targeting baby boomers, you may find that as they grow older, there are not enough younger people replacing them to sustain your business.

Estimating Profitability

$500 Total margin dollars
− $200 Product-related fixed marketing costs
$300 Net contribution to help pay G&A costs

Normally, these amounts would be calculated on an annual basis.

In other words, due to a demographic shift, your market segment will have shrunk.

Another example can be found in the tourism industry. Tourism is vulnerable to gasoline price increases and unfavorable currency exchange rates that can make travel more expensive. If these factors result in a decline in tourist traffic, then tourist-oriented hotels, restaurants, and gift shops may be unable to cover their fixed costs, such as rent and utilities.

The same kind of scenario can apply to your own product. If your market segment shrinks to the point where you are no longer able to cover your fixed costs, then your product will generate a negative net contribution. This will reduce your bottom line profit. Therefore, before you launch a new product, consider not just the size of your target segment, but also its rate of growth or decline.

Factors that Influence Your Profitability

Your firm's profitability will be affected by your own management decisions. But it will also be affected by aspects of your business environment that you cannot control. The most important influences may include the intensity of competition, the size of your market segment, and the price sensitivity of your customers. These factors are often closely interrelated. For instance, the larger your segment, the greater your potential sales volume will be. However, a larger segment may attract more rivals, and this will give your customers more alternatives to choose from. The more alternatives your customers have to choose from, the more price-sensitive they may be. To overcome their price sensitivity, you may need a lower price, or more advertising and promotion, or product positioning that is more distinctive.

If you reduce your price, you'll cut into your per unit margins. But a lower price may also enable you to achieve a higher sales volume. This may yield a higher total contribution margin. A higher sales volume may also help you lower your production cost per unit.

Does this seem complicated? Well, it is. But here are two simple rules that you should follow if you want to maximize your profits:

- Always set your price to maximize your total margin dollars (total contribution margin). In other words, cut your price only if you believe that your sales volume will increase enough to more than compensate for your lost per-unit margin.
- Always try to maximize your product's net contribution. To do this, you may need to carefully control your marketing costs. But remember that without marketing research, advertising, and sales commissions, your product may not sell at all. Hence, you should cut only whatever costs are unnecessary.

Note that these rules do not apply if your overriding objective is to maximize market share, and you are not concerned about short-term profitability.

In any case, in the long run, your total margin dollars must exceed your product's fixed costs. To achieve this, you will need at least enough customers to break even. So an important first step on the road to success is to verify that your prospective target segment is actually large enough to be profitable.

> When your total margin dollar amount equals your product's fixed costs, your product is breaking even. What is your **break even sales volume**? It is the number of products you must sell to earn sufficient total margin dollars to pay for your product's fixed costs. Your **break even sales volume** = (your product's fixed costs) / (your contribution margin per unit)

Chapter 8

Secure a Strategic Advantage

Having the best product on the market can be an important advantage. But having the best product is rarely enough. Your product also needs to be distinctively positioned with an effective marketing mix, targeted at a suitable, worthwhile segment.

In addition, you should understand all of your possible sources of competitive advantage, in order to make the best of your circumstances. Your sources of competitive advantage should be considered carefully, before you enter a market – even while your new products are still in the development stage.

Gunther's TuneIn cosmic radio receiver has remained in the development stage for three years at a cost of $30 million. Designed for use by consumers who wish to enjoy radio broadcasts emanating from planets in distant galaxies, TuneIn radios represent a radical innovation in technology and entertainment. With their initial development complete, they are now ready to enter the introduction stage of the product life cycle (PLC), during which Gunther will start promoting and selling them to his target market.

Skim Pricing

Confident that he is at least two years ahead of his rivals, Gunther is planning to employ a **skim pricing** strategy. That is, he will introduce his radios at high prices, and sell them to the most eager customers, known as **innovators**. Because they are so eager to try out new products, innovators tend to be not very price-sensitive. However, this tiny market of enthusiasts will eventually become saturated, once all customers interested in the product have purchased it. Then, Gunther will gradually reduce his prices, to make his radios affordable for progressively larger and more price-sensitive segments of the market.

> The first customers to purchase a product soon after it is launched are known as **innovators**. Following them are the **early adopters**. Eager to try new products, both groups tend to be less price-sensitive than later customers. Innovators and early adopters also tend to have more experience with new products. Their experience can earn them respect as **opinion leaders**. Consequently, they may play an important role in influencing subsequent consumers' purchase decisions. These subsequent segments include the **early majority**, then the **late majority**, and finally, the **laggards**.

Gunther believes his skim pricing strategy is viable because, for the first two years after his product launch, he will face no price competition. In the absence of any competition, he will be able to earn high unit margins. But his total margin dollars will be limited by his low initial sales volume.

One advantage of skim pricing is that, by starting with a low volume, Gunther will have a chance to iron out any technical wrinkles in his product design or manufacturing processes, while still operating on a small scale. He could also manufacture at a low enough volume to cause artificial scarcity, possibly enhancing the prestige of owning one of his radios. As well, his first customers are likely to be enthusiasts, willing to provide valuable feedback on how to improve his radios, before he starts large-scale mass production. They would also tend to be **opinion leaders**. That is, because enthusiasts tend to be knowledgeable in their field of interest, their opinions are valued and respected by other less-informed consumers. A favorable attitude toward his radios among opinion leaders could therefore work to Gunther's advantage.

If Gunther's early customers are really thrilled with his TuneIn radios, they could become **brand evangelists**. In other words, they could become so excited about his radios that they might actively try to persuade other consumers to purchase them. To consumers, this kind of **word-of-mouth advertising** can seem more credible and unbiased than paid advertising. Word-of-mouth advertising costs nothing, though you may need to wait patiently for it to spread among your target consumers.

Penetration Pricing

More aggressive than skim pricing, **penetration pricing** involves setting a low initial price for your product, with the aim of rapidly gaining market share. It can help you compete with any rivals that are present in your market at the start of your product life cycle. In that case, one of your top priorities should be to win new customers as quickly as possible.

This is especially true if your product is normally purchased repeatedly or by subscription. If so, any customers who become loyal to your rivals may be impossible to win back. So you should attract new customers as quickly as possible. Penetration pricing can be one way to accomplish that.

Gunther could employ a penetration pricing strategy by setting low initial prices – perhaps even lower than his initial per-unit cost. Why would he sell his radios for less than it costs to make them? He might do this in anticipation of a lower per-unit cost he expects to achieve in the near future, when he reaches a higher volume of sales. He was recently overheard making the following comment: "Our production costs are $100 per radio right now. But once we achieve a high sales volume, we'll be manufacturing our radios at $20 each. If we start selling our radios at $50 each right from the start, we'll encounter a lot less price resistance from consumers, and we'll reach our high-volume target much more quickly. Initially, we will be losing money on every radio sold. But as we reach a higher sales and production volume, our costs will decline sharply, and we will become profitable."

While Gunther's strategy makes sense, there is some risk in it: He might not ever be able to reduce his costs enough to earn acceptable profit margins. If he cannot lower his costs as much as he anticipates, then his product might remain unprofitable. He may eventually be forced to raise his prices, possibly costing his firm some market share and credibility.

Low Cost Barriers Can Discourage Rivals

An important advantage of penetration pricing is that it can dissuade potential rivals from entering your market. This can be achieved if your low prices convince your rivals that your market would be unprofitable for them.

Gunther is counting on eventually reaching high enough sales and production volumes to attain economies of scale that his rivals cannot hope to match. While he has considered penetration pricing to accomplish this quickly, he still prefers the skim pricing approach. Skim pricing will allow him to build his business slowly and carefully. As he gradually lowers his prices, his sales and production volumes will increase. This will allow his per-unit production costs to decline. And that will eventually allow him to price his products aggressively enough to deter his rivals' entry into the market.

However, Gunther will need to achieve this within the next two years. Then, when his rivals are ready to enter the market, they will be confronted with his low cost barrier. In other words, they will find it difficult to reach a high enough sales volume to match his low production costs. This is because, by the time they enter the market, his brand will be well-established – known and trusted by consumers – and will be difficult to dislodge. He will enjoy a dominant market share, and a powerful low-cost advantage.

If his rivals have no realistic prospect of matching Gunther's low costs, then they may be forced to price their products higher, which will further limit their market penetration. Foreseeing this scenario, they will likely feel reluctant to enter the market at all. Thus, Gunther's low production costs will have functioned as an effective entry barrier.

A low cost of production is a barrier that you too can erect to deter competitor entry into your own market. You can achieve low production costs by manufacturing in large volumes. That is, if your firm dominates a market, you will have the largest sales and production volume, and therefore the greatest economies of scale. You will also acquire greater experience, enabling you to operate with greater efficiency.

If your costs are the lowest, then you can undercut your rivals' prices if you choose to. Alternatively, you can plough your greater total contribution margin back into product development and advertising. This will help to perpetuate your competitive advantage.

However, economies of scale are not the only way to achieve low production costs. Your rivals may compensate for your economies of scale by paying lower wages to their employees; by motivating their workforce more effectively; by adopting advanced technologies to efficiently manage their production, quality control, and inventory; by winning government subsidies; or by controlling their fixed costs. To deny them any cost advantage, you will need to operate efficiently and effectively in every possible way.

Segment More Finely

Another way to circumvent low-cost barriers is to segment your market more finely. For example, Gunther's current radios are targeted broadly to customers with a variety of different musical tastes. His technology allows reception of radio signals from three distant planets that broadcast classical, country, and rock music respectively. But since most consumers are interested in just one of these musical styles, they tend to feel that they are being forced to pay for radio stations that they do not want. Rock music fans are simply not interested in alien opera.

Addressing this concern, a rival firm, Solar Sonic, has recently announced plans to market a more specialized RockRadio that will receive just rock music broadcasts – from ten different planets. With its more focused positioning, this radio receiver will likely be more satisfying for rock music fans. In other words, Solar Sonic is segmenting the market more finely, to attract Gunther's rock music customers. And by preemptively announcing their product two years in advance, Solar Sonic may have persuaded many rock fans to postpone their purchase of a cosmic radio until the RockRadio is available.

This preemptive tactic is a serious concern for Gunther, because the rock music segment makes up roughly one third of his market. If he loses these customers, his sales volume will be cut drastically, and he will not be able to achieve the low production costs he has been counting on.

Low Cost or Finer Segmentation?

To counter the Solar Sonic threat, Gunther is wondering whether he should make three specialized radio models, each configured for just one kind of music: either classical, or country, or rock. Each of these radios would be simpler to make, and thus would require fewer components. This would reduce production costs. At the same time, unfortunately, Gunther would lose economies of scale, as he would be manufacturing in smaller batches. Overall, the cost savings of having fewer components would be largely eliminated by the lost economies of scale. Nonetheless, his customers would be more satisfied because they could purchase a radio model more closely tailored to their specific needs. Classical connoisseurs would get just classical music, country buffs would get just country music, and rock aficionados would get just rock music. By sacrificing his economies of scale in favor of finer segmentation, Gunther would hope to block the Solar Sonic threat. However, he has not yet made a decision, and is still considering his options.

In some situations, the trade-off between economies of scale and finer segmentation is less ambiguous. For example, if Kevin baked 1000 identical cookies in one single batch, his cost-per-cookie would be much lower than if he baked ten different batches of 100 cookies each. That's because mixing the ingredients for one large batch would be much less time-consuming than mixing the ingredients for 10 different smaller batches. Hence, segmenting his market more finely would result in a higher production cost per cookie, which would inevitably be reflected in higher selling prices for consumers.

Profit from Customer Retention

Cost-effectiveness is always a priority in business. One of the best ways to operate cost-effectively is to retain your existing customers. That way, you can spread the cost of acquiring each customer over more sales. Of course, it's easier to retain customers if your product line attracts repeat purchases.

Knowing this, Gunther has decided to design his radios to accept software and hardware upgrades. The software upgrades will be downloadable from his website at a reasonable cost. And his radios will accept up to 10 hardware expansion modules that can be snapped in, to increase each radio's reception capabilities.

Gunther believes that the flexibility of his radio technology will help assuage customer concerns that a newly purchased radio might rapidly become obsolete. And hopefully, the periodic release of software and hardware upgrades in coming years will sustain consumer excitement about his radios, retain his customers, and generate ongoing revenue streams.

Retain Your Customers with Switching Costs

With some products, customers face switching costs arising from the nature of the product itself. For example, customers who have already learned how to use one kind of word processing software may feel that too much effort would be required to switch to a competing brand. This is a *natural* switching cost.

Microsoft has attempted to overcome this kind of switching cost by adding special features to their word-processing software – known as Word® – to ensure a smooth transition for customers who switch from WordPerfect®, which is a competing product.

In contrast, *artificial* switching costs are not inherent in the product itself. They are created solely to reward and encourage customer loyalty. For example, airline companies issue travel credits – frequent flyer points – based on the distance flown by their customers.

Switching costs can help you retain satisfied customers. But if switching costs are employed to entrap *dissatisfied* customers, these customers can become resentful, and eager to escape from your brand at the first opportunity. This can happen with cell-phone contracts, Internet access contracts, or home mortgages, for example. Therefore, to avoid resentment, it's best to use switching costs in conjunction with a very responsive customer satisfaction program.

Offer a Community They Can Belong To

One way to create switching costs is to establish a community to which your customers can feel they belong. Many customers enjoy feeling involved in a community. They like to feel they can make a contribution, whether by providing technical advice to other community members, or by making new product suggestions. Their sense of community can result in greater enthusiasm for your products and loyalty to your firm. You can create a community by organizing an online fan club, or setting up an Internet discussion forum.

Perfect Your Product

To attract and retain customers, it's essential that you offer a satisfying product. To do this, you may need to continue improving your product over time. This will be especially true immediately after your product's initial launch, if it still has some rough edges. The newness of your product may attract innovators and early adopters, who value novelty over reliability and ease of use. But to please the wider market of more conservative consumers, you will need to refine your product, and ensure that it is dependable and user-friendly.

This is much like the challenge faced by early makers of computer hardware and software. After their initial product launch, they typically still needed some years of further product refinement to achieve the ease of use and reliability required for acceptance by the general public. In fact, in fast-changing technology markets, ongoing continuous product refinement can be a crucial strategic advantage.

Thwart Imitation

Are products in your category expensive to develop? Rivals may be reluctant to enter your market if they are unsure of being able to recover their product development costs.

On the other hand, if your rivals are able to learn from your mistakes, or reverse-engineer your product, or leapfrog your technology, they may be able to enter your market with a much lower R&D investment than yours. If learning from you enables them to lower their R&D investment, they may be able to significantly undercut your prices.

To legally protect a new product or technology, you can attempt to secure a patent. But rivals may find ingenious ways to circumvent your patents, and imitate your products anyway. Or they may offer similar benefits by other means. So you should go further than merely preventing imitation. You should erect a number of different complementary barriers. For example, in addition to high R&D investment barriers, you may also benefit from low-cost barriers, high brand awareness, widespread distribution, long-term sales contracts, and coordinated strategic networks.

Devious Entry Strategies for Latecomers

Gunther remains concerned that Solar Sonic might find other ways to circumvent his entry barriers. Perhaps they could leapfrog his technology with further radical innovations. Though Gunther might want to adopt a new technology in response, he could experience mixed motives about that, feeling reluctant to abandon his investment in his existing technology and production facilities.

As late entrants, Gunther's rivals may be able to benefit from observing his mistakes. They could also benefit from his efforts to educate consumers about how much fun it is to own a cosmic radio receiver. Or they could form alliances with cable TV networks for alternative modes of cosmic radio broadcast reception. Thus, while industry pioneers normally have the strongest position, latecomers can sometimes seize unexpected advantages.

Tie Up Scarce Resources

Tying up scarce resources is a tactic some firms use to block their rivals. Gunther has taken steps to tie up scarce resources that his rivals will need to operate in the cosmic radio industry. He has purchased Moon Metal Mining Ltd., the only company holding the rights to mine the lunar minerals that are essential for cosmic radio technology. And for three years now, he has been hiring the best and brightest radio engineers available.

Show Serious Commitment

To discourage his rivals, Gunther has publicly announced his intention to construct a massive production facility for his radio receivers. This irreversible investment should convince his potential rivals of his absolute commitment to the market. They will no doubt appreciate that any competitor who lacks an escape from the market will be motivated to fight relentlessly, no matter how dire the circumstances. This will make the prospect of competing with Galactic all the more intimidating.

The broad group of all firms with which you cooperate closely – including allied firms, suppliers, intermediaries, advertising agencies, and consultants – is known as your **strategic network**. By comparison, your **supply chain** is limited to the firms that help you procure raw materials and distribute finished products. This normally includes just your suppliers and intermediaries.

Coordinate Your Strategic Network

You can gain another powerful advantage by building a well-coordinated **strategic network**. By working closely with other firms, you may be able to achieve results that your rivals cannot imitate. For example, Microsoft and Intel coordinated their software and hardware development with each other to secure strong positions in their respective markets. No doubt, their business relationship comprised just one component in each firm's entire strategic network.

Take Advantage of Network Effects

By coordinating with other firms, you may be able to develop a strategic network advantage. A similar term – network effects – refers to something quite different. The advantages of network effects are derived from achieving a critical mass of members in a network. To understand this, consider an old-fashioned marketplace.

When buyers and suppliers congregate to trade, they form a marketplace. The more buyers and suppliers in the marketplace, the more opportunities there are to do business. The marketplace increases in value to its members as the number of members increases. As people gravitate to the existing market, rival markets become more difficult to establish. This phenomenon, known as **network effects**, is illustrated by the snowballing of YouTube's user community. Because network effects block rivals so effectively, they can provide an enduring competitive advantage.

A similar effect can influence the adoption of technology standards, such as the VHS video format, and music CDs. As more firms adopt a new technology standard, more customers are attracted to it, which in turn attracts more firms. This tends to block competing standards, even if they are technically superior.

Other Barrier Advantages

You can erect additional entry barriers by building a strong brand, advertising heavily, or developing close customer relationships and loyalty. With sufficient political clout, you may even be able to lobby the government to regulate the industry in your favor.

Efficiency, Innovation, or Relationships?

Another approach to achieving a competitive advantage is to focus on at least one of three fundamental strategic positions: efficiency, innovation, or customer relationship excellence. Wal-Mart is the epitome of efficiency and low cost. In contrast, Apple Inc. stands for innovation. Virgin Atlantic Airways is known for their exceptional customer relationships, having gone to great lengths to offer a stress-free travel experience. Amazon.com has combined efficient, innovative operations with a strong customer relationship focus to prosper in the mature book retail business. Dell has succeeded in the maturing personal computer market through innovative mass-customization technology. This has enabled them to build close customer relationships while offering innovative computer products at low prices.

The strategies outlined in this chapter can be employed by both you and your rivals. So who will gain the advantage? Most likely, the edge will go to whichever firm demonstrates the most ingenuity in strategy selection and execution.

Chapter 9

Pricing Strategies Simplified

What pricing strategy should you employ when launching a new product? Two common strategies are *skim pricing* and *penetration pricing*. Because skim pricing entails setting high initial prices that earn high unit margins, it can allow you to be profitable even at a low initial sales volume. But can you convince your innovators and early adopters that your new product is so much better than any competing alternatives that it's worth a premium price? And do you need a gradual product introduction to allow enough time to refine your technology, your design, or your manufacturing processes? If not, then *penetration pricing* may be more suitable, provided that:
- Your product is fully developed and market-tested
- You are prepared to manufacture and market your product in high volume
- Your customers are price-sensitive
- Your product faces significant price competition.

Service Pricing

Can skim pricing be a useful strategy for a service business? It seems unlikely. Skim pricing might make sense if you can realistically expect to reduce your costs over time. Product businesses typically can lower their costs as they gradually achieve manufacturing economies of scale. But service businesses are different. They are more labor-intensive. Their biggest expense is likely to remain their hourly wages and salaries, no matter how large they grow. And so economies of scale are harder to achieve. After all, how much can you improve the efficiency of a beautician, a lawyer, or an airline pilot? And since highly-skilled personnel cannot be easily replaced, you may find it impossible to negotiate lower wages.

If you cannot significantly lower the labor costs of your service business, then skim pricing won't make sense. By gradually reducing your prices, you'll only cut into your margins. And there won't be much benefit in reducing your prices anyway, if you are serving repeat customers whose price sensitivity is unlikely to change over time.

This is quite different from a typical skim pricing scenario that involves selling durable products such as new technology televisions at high initial prices to a segment that becomes saturated after the customers have purchased just once. Successively lower prices are then used to target the remaining more price-sensitive segments.

What if your service business has the potential to achieve low costs? And what if you want to reach a large sales volume in a price-sensitive market? In this case, *penetration* pricing might be a good choice. For example, a chain of budget hairstyling outlets could benefit from a penetration pricing strategy, if it can recruit less-qualified employees at lower wages and train them to offer a limited number of hairstyles.

In any business, efficiency can be an important way to control costs. To operate a *service* business efficiently, you can standardize procedures, adopt efficient technologies, and assign routine tasks to less-skilled employees. This latter approach is common among auto repair shops that specialize in muffler or tire replacement. The easier tasks are assigned to the less-skilled lower-wage employees, to save on labor costs.

Another approach to lowering service business costs is to motivate your personnel more effectively. You can encourage pride in your firm. You can publicly recognise outstanding achievement. And you can promote team cohesion, trust, and coordination. These measures may cause your team's productivity to increase, effectively lowering your labor costs.

> Some firms operate with minimal physical facilities. For example, a language translation firm can operate from a single small office, if they employ translators who work at home only when needed. Thus, their production capacity is flexible. Other firms require substantial **fixed capacity**. This refers to physical facilities that cannot be easily converted to other uses. Car manufacturing plants and restaurants are examples.

One essential distinction between products and services is that products can be manufactured in advance, and stored for later use. By contrast, services cannot be stored, as they are transitory and must be consumed when they are provided. For instance, empty seats in movie theaters and on airplanes are wasted inventory. Saddled with **fixed capacity**, service firms such as these typically attempt to smooth fluctuations in demand by varying their prices. Discounted prices are offered when demand is low, to attract enough customers to at least cover fixed costs. This is a tactic employed by hotels and vacation resorts when they offer lower prices during quiet seasons. However, if your customers are unlikely to respond to lower prices, then discounting will only hurt your margins without increasing your sales volume.

Fluctuating demand can also result in wasted payroll costs, if your employees are left idle during slow periods. One way to minimize this kind of waste is to encourage customers to serve themselves, so that fewer employees are needed. In other words, the necessary labor is available only when needed, because the customers themselves provide it. This self-serve approach is common among gas stations and discount retailers. By detaching their service from the products they sell, firms that use this approach are able to minimize the cost of idle employees, and this allows them to keep their prices low.

Common Pricing Strategies

Whether you sell tangible products, or intangible services, your pricing strategies should be consistent with the rest of your marketing mix. For example, if your price is high, then your product should be of high quality. Moreover, your advertising and choice of distribution channels should be consistent with your high price and quality. Of course, your pricing should also offer good value, as perceived by your customers. And your pricing must allow your firm to operate profitably.

As you read through the following pricing strategy descriptions, consider which ones would be most suitable for your business.

Prestige Pricing

Prestige pricing involves setting high prices as an indicator of prestige and quality. Of course, the actual quality of the product must meet expectations.

Bundle Pricing

Several products can be sold together and priced specially as a bundle. For example, a computer can be sold with bundled software, to encourage customers to adopt software programs that they might not otherwise consider. However, some customers may want to purchase the products separately. If you don't make your products available separately for them, then your rivals may step in to satisfy the need. So if you want to bundle your products, consider making them available separately as well.

Reference Pricing

Reference pricing involves comparing your price to your product's regular price, or the price of competing products.

Value Pricing

Value pricing entails recognizing the value your customers perceive in your product, and then pricing your product accordingly, regardless of your cost.

Dynamic Pricing

Every time I look up the airfare, the price has changed. What's going on?

Dynamic pricing entails frequently adjusting prices to smoothen demand. A computer program can be set to lower prices when lower demand is detected, so that demand is stimulated. Frequent price changes have the added advantage of thwarting consumer price comparisons across rival firms.

Two-Part Pricing

Warehouse shopping clubs charge an annual fee, and also earn a profit on everything they sell. This is known as two-part pricing. It can encourage customers to shop regularly in order to justify their annual fees. Many golf clubs operate the same way, charging annual membership fees, as well as usage fees. Having paid their annual fees, members are more inclined to use the golf course, racking up more usage charges. Besides encouraging members to use the course, the annual membership fees are a stable source of revenue that can help the club reliably cover their fixed costs.

Everyday Low Pricing

Cost Plus Pricing

We need a 25% margin on everything we sell. It's up to the manufacturer to set a reasonable price. We just take our usual cut.

Cost plus pricing involves adding a set percentage to the cost of each item that is sold, regardless of the value perceived by customers. Its strength is its simplicity and ease of administration. But its weakness is that it ignores the potential to charge more in some circumstances, and the need to charge less in others. Nonetheless, it is often the most practical pricing method for wholesalers and retailers who carry a broad assortment of goods.

Chapter 10

Treacherous Distribution Channel Dynamics

No matter what business you're in, you'll need to perform some basic marketing tasks, such as segmenting your market, and positioning your product.

As well as tasks like these, if you work with tangible products, there is another area of marketing activity that can be particularly important: The design and management of your distribution channels. Your distribution channels consist of all the wholesalers, retailers, and other companies that help you make your product conveniently available for purchase by your final customers. An understanding of distribution channels can be vital to your success, whether you mass-produce your own products, or resell products made by other firms.

Channel Jargon

Learning about distribution channels requires a knowledge of some basic terminology. Let's cover some of it now. A **distribution channel** consists of a particular set of **intermediaries**, or middleman. Wholesalers and distributors purchase goods from manufacturers – or from each other. Then they sell the goods to retailers, who sell them to consumers. Thus, wholesalers, distributors, and retailers are known as *intermediaries*.

Any intermediaries who buy and sell from each other are known collectively as a **distribution channel**. For example, traditional book wholesalers and retailers would together comprise one distribution channel. As an alternative, if giftware wholesalers and retailers also carry books, then they would comprise another distribution channel.

Some channel terminology – such as the terms **wholesaler** and **distributor** – can have different meanings in different industries. In this book, these two terms are used interchangeably.

Other intermediary types can include **brokers** and **agents**. These intermediaries arrange transactions without taking possession of the goods. Their income is normally earned as commissions. In contrast, distributors, wholesalers, and retailers earn their income by marking up the price of the products that they buy and sell.

What is Your Channel Structure?

The type and number of intermediaries used by a manufacturer is known as its **channel structure**. You should design your channel structure with care, to ensure effective distribution for your products. For example, a bakery could sell directly to a grocery store, or it could also sell through food wholesalers. These are two different channel design choices that will affect product availability, pricing, and sales effort.

Sometimes manufacturers sell directly to their final customers, without the help of any intermediaries at all. This channel structure is known as **direct distribution**. Dell is one company that sells its own products directly to consumers, both over the phone, and over the Internet. Dell's direct distribution channel structure has been one of the firm's key success factors. Similarly, your own channel structure may have a crucial, long-term impact on your business. For this reason, you should take great care when making channel design decisions.

On the other hand, in certain industries, you may have little or no influence on the structure of your distribution channel. For example, if you operate a traditional restaurant, then you will inevitably sell your food directly to your customers – without the help of any intermediaries. Or if you operate a fast-food outlet as a franchisee, purchasing food ingredients supplied by a franchisor, then you are an intermediary in a pre-defined channel structure. However, even if you cannot influence your own channel structure, you will find that a knowledge of distribution channels can help you understand your industry, which can help you make better business decisions.

If you are in the business of mass-producing items for sale, whether farm products, children's clothing, or consumer electronics, then you will need to utilize distribution channels. They will enable you to access a market large enough to consume all of the products you make. But distribution channel intermediaries do not work free of charge. If you are using wholesalers or retailers, you will need to discount your prices when you sell to them, so that they can earn enough margin to cover their costs and earn a profit.

While the percentage margin can vary widely across industries, retailers often need a 40% discount, while distributors earn about 25%. Therefore, if the suggested retail price for your product is $100, you will have to sell to your distributors at $45. That is, $100 × (1 − 0.40) × (1 − 0.25) = $45. In other words, $100 minus a 40% discount leaves $60, and $60 minus a 25% discount leaves $45. You may also have to pay the cost of freight to your wholesalers. And you may need to refund the cost of any overstock that they cannot sell.

When you consider how much it costs to sell through intermediaries, you might be tempted to bypass them altogether, in order to earn higher margins. This can make sense in some circumstances. For instance, you might choose to sell direct over the Internet to individuals who are not able to obtain your product locally. Or you might decide to bypass your wholesalers and sell directly to a large retail chain – if their sales volume is sufficient to compensate for the extra services they will require. For example, your sales reps may need to regularly visit each of your retailer's locations across an entire continent to check and replenish their stock. The advantages would include a higher profit margin, and hopefully a better understanding of your customers' needs. However, this would be an expensive undertaking, and would also consume considerable management time and effort.

In many circumstances, the services offered by intermediaries will prove crucial to the success of your product. Moreover, your intermediaries are likely to do their job better than you could do it, because they specialize in their role. Wholesalers in particular can simplify distribution and achieve greater efficiency, as shown in the accompanying diagram.

What Consumers Want

To understand how intermediaries can help your business, try to imagine a consumer's perspective. Individual consumers will typically make most of their purchases in physical retail locations, known as **bricks and mortar stores (BAM stores)**. These stores operate from a physical address, as opposed to selling over the Internet. In BAM stores, customers can browse a large assortment of merchandise in a pleasant shopping ambience. They can discover your product, inspect it, obtain sales help, and perhaps negotiate financing. Then they can purchase your

Intermediaries Simplify Distribution

Intermediaries can simplify distribution by reducing the number of relationships that must be maintained. In the upper diagram, 48 relationships are required for three manufacturers to sell directly to 16 retailers. In the lower diagram, the use of a wholesaler reduces that number to just 19 relationships, thereby increasing efficiency.

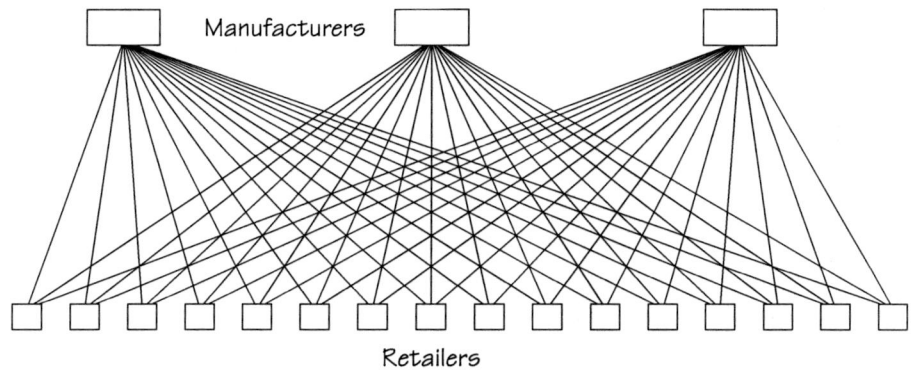

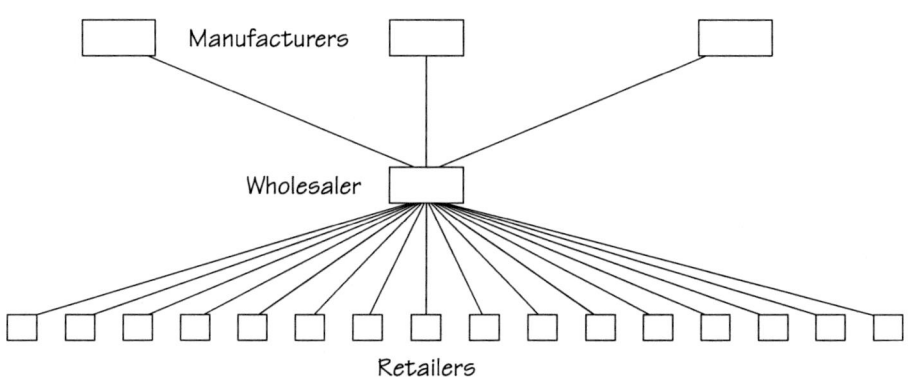

product in whatever small quantity suits their needs, and take it home immediately, without having to wait for it to arrive in the mail.

Providing this kind of shopping experience is beyond the capabilities of most manufacturers. Yet this is the kind of shopping experience that most consumers want. If your product is not available in this kind of convenient, attractive shopping environment, your potential customers may not discover or purchase it at all.

Instead of BAM stores, some consumers prefer printed catalogs or the Internet, for the convenience of shopping at home at any hour of the day or night. The Internet is also ideal for consumers seeking hard-to-find items, such as books and music CDs. To satisfy this need, online retailers can serve an entire country from as little as one location. With an entire country ordering from just one location, even relatively unpopular items can turn over often enough to make stocking them economical. This can make it practical for an Internet retailer to stock a very broad assortment of items, increasing their website's attractiveness for online shoppers.

Everyone Prefers Convenient Purchasing

Consumers tend to prefer outlets that sell a *broad assortment* of merchandise. This is because they appreciate the convenience of *one-stop shopping*. Here's a hypothetical example: Cecilia Smith, a mother of 3 children, is among the almost 1% of the population who suffer from celiac disease. This is an autoimmune reaction to gluten, which is a protein found in wheat, rye, barley, and oats. Unfortunately, her local Humongous Discount Grocer is not interested in devoting 2 square feet of shelf space to stocking breakfast cereals that are free from gluten. And so Cecilia spends her *entire* family food budget at the more expensive Specialty Foods outlet, which does stock gluten-free cereal, but is 5 kilometers further from Cecilia's home. She is willing to travel this extra distance and pay more because she is a busy mom who has only enough time to make one food-shopping trip each week. If Humongous continues to ignore the needs of Cecilia and other customers like her, they could lose a significant share of the market to more responsive grocery chains.

Some retailers cannot offer a broad selection, because their space really is too limited. Instead, their strength may be the convenience of their location, the speed of their service, or the attractiveness of their discount prices. But other retailers do offer a broad selection, and this entails purchasing goods produced by a number of different manufacturers. However, ordering from many different manufacturers can become an overwhelming, time-consuming chore. It can distract retailers from their core business of presenting and selling merchandise. For this reason, just as consumers prefer shops that carry a broad assortment of goods, many retailers likewise prefer wholesalers that offer a broad assortment. This can allow them to deal with fewer vendors, which can reduce paperwork and simplify operations. Thus, if retailers cannot purchase your product through their favorite wholesalers, they may not bother carrying it at all.

Choose Appropriate Intermediaries

If convenient one-stop shopping is so appealing, why don't most local grocery stores carry a comprehensive selection of consumer electronics? Consumers would undoubtedly find it more convenient to purchase electronics without having to travel further than their local grocer. But even the few grocers who do carry electronics do not typically carry a broad selection. Why?

The reason for this is that grocers prefer items – like groceries – that they can price competitively to sell in substantial volume with minimal sales assistance. This is their normal mode of business. But only the most popular, budget-priced consumer electronics products meet these criteria. Other consumer electronics products are just too complex or expensive, and sell too slowly. For example, a sophisticated high-end digital camera would require more sales and technical expertise than would typically be found among grocery store employees. Such a camera would also sell slowly, necessitating a higher price and higher profit margin to compensate for the slow turnover. A high price would conflict with the low-price positioning of most grocery stores. And so if a grocery supermarket carries any electronics at all, their selection will likely be limited to the simplest, most popular models – items that can be priced aggressively to sell in high volume, with minimal sales assistance.

A better choice of intermediaries for a high-end digital camera would be specialty camera shops staffed with more knowledgeable salespeople. Such specialty retailers would likely be fewer in number. Each of them would draw customers from a larger geographic area, enabling them to achieve an acceptable turnover rate for their inventory. And with their greater expertise, these specialty shops would sell high-end cameras more successfully.

This illustrates how an appropriate choice of intermediaries can help you achieve more effective distribution for your product.

Avoid the Free-Riding Trap

Free-riding is a kind of consumer behavior that can cause your intermediaries to turn against you. Here's how it works:

A low-service discount outlet that retails a high-end camera would likely make only a minimal personal selling effort. And so their cost of selling the camera would be lower than the personal selling costs incurred by a full-service camera shop. This would enable the discount outlet to undercut the full-service camera store's price.

Consequently, a customer could benefit from a lengthy demonstration of the camera's features at the camera shop, and then visit the discount store or website to purchase the item more economically. In effect, the customer would have obtained the camera shop's educational service without paying for it.

Discouraged and angered with customers repeatedly **free-riding** in this manner, the camera shop would be inclined to discontinue selling any models sold by the discount store. Without adequate sales effort, the sales of the camera might decline across all outlets, and even the discount store could eventually lose interest.

Feeling bitter about having been exposed to such unfair competition, the camera shop owners might thereafter shun the manufacturer's entire line of products. Thus, the manufacturer would lose a valuable retailer.

The above story is an example of **channel conflict**. You should try to avoid serious channel conflict of this kind, because it can turn your channel members against your product – and your firm. If you lose the support of your channel members, they can switch their customers to your rivals' products, or drop your product altogether. In either case, your sales will dwindle.

Therefore, if you decide to use high-service channels to sell a complex or expensive product, do not undermine their effort by also making the product available through low-service discount outlets.

As an exception to this rule, you can sell through incompatible channels if they serve entirely different markets. For example, if you sell through a wholesale club that serves only its members, their limited market might not significantly overlap the market served by your high-service intermediaries.

Your channel members will enthusiastically support your product only if they believe they will be fairly compensated for the services they provide. From their point of view, every product they carry must generate some profit margin to help pay for the cost of their physical facilities, employee payroll, insurance, financing, and advertising. Free-riding can deprive them of the profit margin they need to survive. Likewise, excessive competition can drive the price of your product down to the point where attractive margins can no longer be earned. If this happens, your channel members will lose their motivation to sell your product.

When to use Intensive Distribution

Some products, such as grocery items and other **fast-moving consumer goods**, require little or no personal selling effort. For this reason, they can be made available in a large number of outlets, for convenient availability. This is known as **intensive distribution**. These goods can be distributed intensively because, without any personal selling effort, free-riding cannot occur. Without any potential for free-riding, these products are unlikely to provoke channel conflict. For fast moving consumer goods, the advantage of intensive distribution is that greater availability tends to increase sales, by offering more convenience for consumers.

In contrast, products that require significant personal selling effort are likely to trigger channel conflict if they are distributed too intensively. Because these products can be complex and expensive, salespeople typically need to spend considerable time and effort explaining them to customers. If these products are available too widely, high-service outlets may feel that their effort is being undermined, and so may prefer to put their effort into selling something else.

Selective & Exclusive Distribution Compared

If you limit the availability of your product to certain chosen intermediaries, then you are employing what is known as **selective distribution**. If you go a step further and limit the availability of your product to just one intermediary per geographic territory, then you are employing **exclusive distribution**. These two forms of limited distribution can help motivate your intermediaries, by assuring them that they will not be exposed to excessive price competition and free-riding. And so they will tend to feel that it is worthwhile to carry your product and put some effort into selling it.

While selective and exclusive distribution are similar in that they limit the availability of your product, they differ in one important respect: Selective distribution will result in some competition among your intermediaries, whereas exclusive distribution will not. That is, with selective distribution, you would normally work with several intermediaries in each territory, and they will inevitably compete with each other. Generally, manufacturers prefer selective distribution, because it stimulates some competition. This can motivate intermediaries to try harder, to price competitively, and to not take their customers for granted. By contrast, with exclusive distribution, you would work with just one intermediary per territory, who would have the exclusive right to sell your product.

Sometimes an intermediary will demand an exclusive territory – for valid reasons. One possible reason could be that their market would be too small to support more than one intermediary. For example, a town of 5,000 people probably could not support two kitchen appliance retailers, each carrying your product line. In this kind of

How Distribution Intensity Affects Intermediary Motivation

Intermediaries tend to be most highly motivated with selective distribution. They can also be motivated by high demand and healthy margins. With exclusive distribution, high motivation is more likely if the intermediary has made substantial investments. Intensive distribution can be tolerated if no personal sales effort is needed.

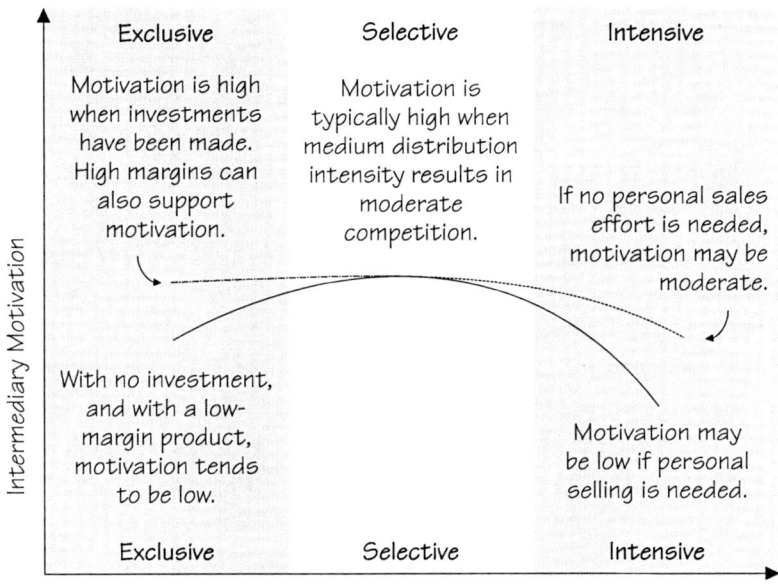

Number of Intermediaries per Territory

situation, to avoid having them both abandon your line in frustration, you should work with just one intermediary on an exclusive basis. But without any competition, how can you be sure that your chosen intermediary will be sufficiently motivated? The most effective approach would be to ensure that your product is competitively priced, and offers your intermediary healthy margins. It should also be supported with a strong brand name, persuasive advertising, and dependable customer service. This approach will motivate your intermediary to sell your product, and will motivate your customers to buy it. In addition, you can offer incentives and bonuses to intermediaries who meet specified sales targets.

Another way to motive an intermediary is to demand that they agree not to carry any products that might compete with yours, in return for territorial exclusivity. This might ensure that their full effort would be devoted to selling your product, instead of its competitors. However, this tactic could have a serious drawback: It could limit your intermediaries' ability to provide the kind of broad assortment that their customers seek. This could weaken your intermediary's market position, and so weaken their ability to sell your product. Therefore, if your product line is not expansive enough by itself to offer a sufficiently broad assortment, then this approach should be avoided.

One of the most compelling reasons for granting an exclusive territory is that your intermediary may need substantial revenues and profits to compensate for having made a large investment in facilities or inventory. For example, car dealers and fast food franchisees must typically invest a considerable sum of money to get started. Inevitably, they will want to feel there is a reasonable prospect of earning an acceptable return on their start-up investment. To achieve this, they may believe it is necessary to secure the exclusive right to sell your product in their territory. In these circumstances, exclusive distribution can make sense. You can be fairly certain that your intermediary will be highly motivated if they have invested a substantial sum of money.

Are there any disadvantages to using selective or exclusive distribution? Yes there are. The main disadvantage is that, with selective or exclusive distribution, your product will be less widely available than it would be with intensive distribution.

However, some products will be sought out by consumers, even without wide availability. If your product is typically a specially-planned purchase of some importance, your customers may be willing to make the necessary shopping effort to obtain it. For example, when shopping for a car, a home stereo, or a high-end digital camera, typical consumers will be sufficiently interested to research the product – perhaps on the Internet – and then seek out whatever specialty retail locations offer informative sales support, or the best price.

Even some impulse items can benefit from limited distribution. This is true if they depend partly on novelty for their appeal, because limited availability can make them seem even more special. Moreover, limited availability can encourage sales effort. Here's an example: Fashionable clothing, jewelry, and home decorative accessories are often purchased on impulse from specialty boutiques. Though these products are not particularly complex, consumers still appreciate sales assistance, for emotional support if nothing else. And so you should distribute these products selectively or exclusively, to encourage the full support of retailers, and to imbue your products with an aura of exclusivity. To compensate for their being available in only a limited number of outlets, you can select outlets located in high-traffic malls or tourist traps, making them easier for consumers to discover.

In contrast, simple, inexpensive products that are purchased routinely should be distributed intensively. If they are not conveniently available, customers may not make any special effort to obtain them. They may instead switch to whatever competing alternative products are on hand. Grocery items are typical examples. Intensive distribution of these products is normally tolerated by intermediaries, as long as they are able to maintain an acceptable volume of sales. And with no need for any significant personal selling effort for these products, there is no opportunity for the kind of customer free-riding that can cause channel conflict.

> **Channel design** is an alternate term for *channel structure*, which is the number and kind of intermediaries through which you distribute your product.

Crucial Channel Design Decisions

No matter what your line of business, one of your most important **channel design** decisions will be whether to adopt intensive, selective, or exclusive distribution. This decision will influence how conveniently your customers will be able to obtain your product. Your distribution intensity decision will also influence how much sales effort you will be able to expect from your intermediaries. Generally, the more intensive your distribution, the less sales effort your intermediaries will be willing to make.

Another important channel design decision you will need to make is whether to sell through wholesalers and retailers, or direct to consumers. One common channel structure involves selling directly to the largest retail chains, while using wholesalers to serve the smaller retail outlets.

Most manufacturers do not sell directly to consumers because they recognize that they lack the necessary retailing expertise and broad product assortment. For this reason, many manufacturer websites intentionally funnel any consumer purchase inquiries to their dealer network.

If you do nevertheless decide to sell your manufactured goods direct to consumers, be careful not to undercut your intermediaries' prices. Otherwise, your intermediaries could feel betrayed or threatened, and might withdraw their support for your products.

On the other hand, by selling direct to customers at fair prices over the Internet, you may be able to exercise some influence over your dealers' pricing. Xerox appears to employ this approach by selling their printers and supplies direct to end-users over the Internet, as well as through local dealers. The advantage seems to be that they can set an upper limit on their dealer's prices, to ensure that their products remain affordable.

Similarly, you may find that, without much competition in a given territory, your dealers may be inclined to raise their prices higher than you would like them to. By selling direct to consumers, you can discourage that. And you can ensure that your customers can easily obtain your products, even if your local dealers are out of stock, or if there are no dealers at all in your customers' vicinity.

Accommodate Diverse Service Needs

Have you ever noticed how some products are typically sold through certain distribution channels? For example, disposable diapers are typically sold in grocery, pharmacy, and discount retail outlets. You'll rarely find them in restaurants, stereo shops and attorney's offices. But there can be significant market segments that deviate from typical purchasing behavior. To reach these segments, you may need to sell through non-standard channels.

For example, computers are typically sold through multiple distribution channels. This is partly because computer literacy varies widely among consumers. Consequently, some consumers will need a great deal of educational sales support, while the more sophisticated consumers will have little or no need for advice. They might prefer to do their own research – about various models of computers, for instance – and then obtain the best possible price by purchasing online, without needing any sales support at all.

In a sense, these customers are easier for a manufacturer to serve, because in the absence of any significant personal selling effort, there is much less potential for channel conflict. So a multi-channel strategy is less risky. Even if these consumers research a product on one retailer's website, and then purchase it on another, the first retailer is unlikely to complain about free-riding, since they have made no personal selling effort. But if you do choose to accommodate these customers by selling on the internet, other customers may free-ride on your high-service BAM retailers, and so some channel conflict may result.

Channel conflict is less likely when your dealers' personal selling effort is normally reciprocated by customer loyalty. For instance, many business customers prefer to purchase their office supplies not from big-box discount stores, but from firms that offer a higher level of service. In this way, these customers can minimize their purchasing effort and avoid being distracted from their work. Because they purchase repeatedly, a mutual understanding can develop between the customer and the supplier. Once a relationship is established, these customers tend to remain loyal, believing that switching would entail too much risk and effort to be worth the bother.

What these examples show is that, to satisfy the diverse service needs of various market segments, you may need to distribute your product through multiple channels. And with a multi-channel strategy, special care will be needed to avoid channel conflict.

The practice of selling through more than one distribution channel is known as **dual distribution**. This term is somewhat confusing because the word *dual* suggests the use of just two distribution channels, whereas in fact the use of three or more channels is also known as dual distribution. A less-confusing alternative term is **multichannel distribution**.

Different Channels for Different Occasions

Selling through multiple distribution channels can enable you to satisfy various segments who have different service needs. Another reason to sell through multiple distribution channels is to satisfy the needs of one particular segment on various different occasions. For example, if you make fruit juice, you might want to sell your product through supermarkets, convenience stores, restaurants, and vending machines. This would allow you to satisfy customers who purchase from vending machines on some occasions, and then at other times consume your product in restaurants, for example.

Selling items such as fruit juice through multiple channels is unlikely to cause channel conflict, whether the product is sold through convenience stores, restaurants, or vending machines. This is because a consumer can enjoy the benefits of a convenience store only by purchasing from a convenience store. Similarly, a consumer can enjoy the service and ambience of a restaurant only by purchasing a meal from the restaurant. Since the service cannot be separated from the product, free-riding is impossible. This is one reason why you are unlikely to encounter much channel conflict when selling simple products like fruit juice through multiple channels.

In summary, there are two main reasons for adopting a multiple-channel distribution strategy:

- To satisfy the needs of different market segments who each prefer to purchase from different outlets

- To make your product available to a particular segment of customers who purchase from different outlets on different occasions.

For your customers, each of your distribution channels offers particular benefits. A bricks and mortar (**BAM**) retailer can offer personal service, in-store ambience, and immediate product availability. In comparison, an Internet retailer can offer 24-hour shopping convenience, a broad assortment of goods, and customer product reviews.

Selling Perishable Goods on the Internet

These days, it's hard to imagine a multi-channel strategy that does not include Internet e-commerce. Even fruit juice is sold on the Internet, though normally by grocery retailers, rather than by juice manufacturers. Consumers appreciate being able to shop for groceries from home at whatever time is convenient. And being able to repeat orders with just a few mouse clicks adds to the appeal.

One reason why grocery retailers can be successful on the Internet is that they can offer the kind of broad product assortment that consumers want. Moreover, if they have store locations near their customers, they can deliver grocery orders quickly. Most manufacturers cannot offer such a wide assortment along with quick delivery, because they carry only their own product lines, and typically lack local distribution centers.

For items that require prompt delivery, such as restaurant food, groceries, and fresh flowers, geographic proximity to customers is important. Food needs to be delivered promptly, when people are hungry. Flowers need to arrive on the appropriate occasion. And anything perishable needs to be delivered speedily, before it spoils.

One way to distribute efficiently from thousands of locations is to establish one national web site that accepts orders, and then route the orders to the nearest local outlet for delivery. For example, a fast-food restaurant chain can establish a single, centralized website for ordering, while for speedy service, each order is actually delivered from the nearest local restaurant. To see how this can work, visit www.pizzapizza.com or www.ftd.com.

Efficient, Economical Internet Channels

Most items sold on the Internet are not perishable. Products that are nonperishable and not too heavy can easily be shipped across a continent or around the world. If they can be purchased online with confidence, then close proximity to customers may not be important.

Therefore, online retailers selling non-perishable items are not limited to serving only their own local market. They can just as easily sell nationally or internationally. Nor are customers limited to buying from local retailers. Thus, online retailers and customers located across an entire continent can now easily do business with each other. Competing across an entire continent puts more pressure on Internet retailers to price their offerings competitively. And they are actually *able* to price competitively because Internet retailing can be more efficient.

> A **pure-clicks retailer** is one that sells only over the internet, ships from a warehouse, and has no bricks-and-mortar retail locations for customers to shop at in person. In contrast, a **bricks-and-clicks retailer** is one that operates both on the Internet, and from a physical storefront location as well.

An online retailer can operate from whatever location is most economical, without needing to lease expensive retail space – in a shopping mall, for example. And an online retailer can achieve economies of scale through rapid inventory turnover by serving an entire continent from just one location. Thus, efficiency and low costs can allow Internet retailers to offer low prices. This can be a powerful advantage over BAM retailers, who are limited to serving just their own local market.

Pure Clicks, or Bricks and Mortar?

Given the advantages enjoyed by Internet retailers, should you abandon your bricks-and-mortar (**BAM**) intermediaries? Probably not. Customers still like to browse, discover, and physically inspect products that interest them – and then take them home immediately. Moreover, many customers value the personal service offered by specialty shops and high-end retailers. This kind of shopping experience is simply not available on the Internet.

Therefore, you may need to utilize both online and BAM channels, in order to satisfy your customers. However, you should try to minimize free-riding, or you could end up suffering the negative effects of channel conflict.

One way to minimize free-riding is to limit product availability to BAM stores, whether or not they also operate online. Even if they operate online, they will be less inclined to drastically discount their online prices, knowing the harm it might cause their own BAM operations. As a result, channel conflict may be avoided.

Despite this logic, some bricks-and-clicks retailers actually do offer greater discounts on their websites, undercutting their own BAM stores. They may do this for several reasons:

- To compete with rival Internet retailers

- To compensate their customers for having to wait for delivery or pay freight charges
- To encourage customers to purchase from their web site, because it is more profitable than their BAM storefronts.

If you are considering limiting your distribution to bricks-and-clicks stores only, you should be aware of a significant drawback to this strategy: It will preclude selling to major *pure-clicks* retailers like Amazon.com. That could limit your sales considerably. In some industries, such as consumer electronics, one way around this problem is to sell one version of your product to your pure-clicks retailers, and a different version to your BAM stores. This can prevent consumers from making direct price comparisons, and so can help prevent free-riding across your distribution channels. But the cost of manufacturing several versions of your product can be prohibitive, if you do not operate on a large scale.

Eliminating channel conflict is a worthy goal, albeit one that can seldom be fully achieved. It will be all the more difficult to achieve if your multi-channel distribution strategy involves selling on the Internet. But if you can find a way to make your product available online without alienating your BAM channels, the Internet can offer an array of marketing opportunities that may be well worth the effort.

Gain an Advantage with Online Communities

If your company has an Internet presence, you may find it advantageous to host an online customer community. For example, both Amazon and Dell allow customers to post their own product reviews and recommendations online. This approach demonstrates respect for customers' opinions, which can encourage involvement and loyalty.

Moreover, customer reviews tend to be perceived as less biased than paid advertising. Consequently, after reading other customers' reviews, a potential customer may be more likely to muster sufficient confidence to proceed with a purchase decision.

Customer communities that are more cohesive and interactive can form around online *user forums*, as can be found on Adobe.com or Corel.com. On these forums, experienced product users advise other users who require assistance. Knowing that such a forum is available should they need it, customers who are considering buying complex products – such as software – may feel more comfortable about making a purchase. The disadvantage of allowing visitor contributions to your website is that you must closely monitor their posts to ensure that nothing is written that would offend other viewers.

Be Careful How You Email Your Customers

One of the great advantages of the Internet is that it allows you to stay in touch with your customers economically via email and your website. For example, Amazon.com asks new customers if they would like to receive periodic emails about special offers. If they agree, then they will occasionally receive emails advertising items that are likely to be of interest, as they are similar to what the customer has previously purchased. This strategy allows Amazon to advertise to their existing customers at practically no cost.

Amazon's permission-based email marketing program illustrates several fundamental principles that you should adhere to when emailing ads to your customers: Amazon's customers can easily withdraw from the program at any time, the emails are sent from a trusted source, and they are not sent so frequently as to become annoying – though this is a matter of personal opinion.

As well, Amazon's advertising emails are tailored to each recipient's interests. In addition, they offer something of value, such as special low prices.

This is very different from the programs offered by some companies that falsely claim to have permission-based email lists for rent. They may claim that, for a fee, they will email your ad to millions of potential customers who supposedly have agreed to receive such ads. Since it may be very difficult to verify the validity of such claims, you should deal only with well-known, reputable firms. If your ad is emailed indiscriminately to individuals and businesses against their wishes, then your advertising will be considered spam, and your company's reputation and goodwill could be seriously damaged. This is not a good way to build strong customer relationships.

Inevitably, the most reliable email advertising list for your business will be a list that your company itself has developed through your own customer transactions. Knowing exactly what each customer on your list has inquired about or purchased from your business will enable you to tailor your advertising messages to their particular needs.

However, this approach will limit your email list to individuals who have already contacted your company. How then can you attract new online customers?

How to Attract Customers on the Internet

One way to attract new customers is to optimize the design and wording of your web pages to achieve a high **ranking** in search engine results. This is known as **search engine optimization,** or **SEO.** For example, if you are selling furniture in Boise, Idaho, then you will want your website to appear at the top of the first **search results page**, when anyone searches for both "furniture" and "Boise" on a **search engine.**

> **Search engines** are web sites like Google.com and Yahoo.com that enable people to look up information on the internet. Based on whatever words are entered by the user, the search engine will produce a listing of relevant web site links, known as **search results**. Your web site's relative position among these results is referred to as your search engine **ranking**. An **organic ranking** is one that is achieved without any payment to the search engine company.

The mechanics of search engine optimization are not very complex. Unfortunately, the results can be unpredictable. This is because the content of other websites may be modified occasionally, which can change their ranking with respect to yours. In addition, search engines sometimes modify their criteria for ranking web sites. So while your website might appear at the top of the first page of search results this week, a few weeks later, your rank may have slipped considerably, with your website appearing toward the bottom of the fifth page instead. On the other hand, the big advantage of search engine optimization is that search engines won't charge you any fees for these **organic results**, and you will need to pay only the cost of modifying your web pages.

Another approach is to *pay* the search engine company for a higher ranking. This is known as **paid placement**. You start by making an informed guess about which search words your customers would likely use, if they were looking for the kinds of products that you sell. Then you would bid on these words, which are also known as *search terms*. For example, you could bid ten cents for two particular words such as "Boise" and "furniture". If your bid exceeds your rivals' bids for the same search terms, then your site will rank higher than theirs every time an Internet user's search terms include both "Boise" and "furniture". If the Internet user then actually clicks on your web site listing, you will have to pay your bid amount to the search engine company. In other words, you can get to the top of the search results page by bidding the highest amount, but you don't have to pay that amount until someone actually clicks on the link to your web site.

A similar concept is **pay-per-click advertising**. This entails paying for your ad to appear on other websites that are relevant to the interests of your target customers. Each time someone clicks on your ad, they are redirected to your own website, where they will hopefully make a purchase.

Both paid placement and pay-per-click advertising can be quite cost-effective. You will typically need to pay only a few cents, each time your listing or ad is clicked. This compares favorably with advertising in traditional media, such as magazines or the radio, which require that you pay for your ad whether anyone notices it or not. Moreover, pay-per-click internet ads bring customers directly to your web site, where they may be able to purchase your goods without any further search effort.

Another major advantage of this kind of advertising is that it can be targeted very precisely. You can target customers according to specific words that they are searching for, or the kinds of websites they are visiting. In addition, the paid placement or pay-per-click company may allow you to set a monthly limit on your advertising budget, so that you don't end up with a bill that is larger than you can afford. As soon as your ad has been clicked enough times to consume your monthly budget, your ad simply stops appearing, and this prevents any further accumulation of click charges.

An appealing online ad, appropriately targeted, may prove highly effective at attracting visitors to your website. But your advertising campaign will be profitable only if you can convert enough of these visitors to paying customers. That will depend on how credible your product seems as a solution to your visitors' needs, how attractively priced it is, and how conveniently you can deliver it. It will also depend on how effectively your website moves your customers through the purchase decision process to a completed purchase transaction.

Your Intermediary Advantage

When designing your channel structure, an important factor to consider is how efficient your various possible intermediaries would be. For example, a particular wholesaler might operate inefficiently because they use poorly-designed inventory management software. If frequent mistakes result, then your retailers may not be able to obtain your product when they need it, and sales will be lost. Or if your intermediaries mark up your product excessively to cover the cost of their inefficiency, your product will be priced less competitively. Rival manufacturers who work with more efficient intermediaries could make their product available to consumers more dependably and at a better price. This would put you at a disadvantage. So choose your intermediaries carefully.

Besides efficiency, another concern is how suitable various distribution channels would be for satisfying your customers in other ways. For example, is it important to your customers that they be able to conveniently return products that they are not satisfied with? Would they prefer to purchase from a high-service retailer, or from a discount outlet on the Internet? Are they prepared to pay more for a sophisticated, elegant shopping ambience? Will a prestige outlet add to the value your customers perceive in your brand? Your answers to questions like these will help you determine the most appropriate intermediaries to work with.

Earn Their Respect and Trust

Whatever channel structure you decide to adopt, you will want to have cordial and productive relations with your intermediaries. This will be easier if you share mutual respect and trust. You can earn their trust by demonstrating fairness, helpfulness, and competence. One way to do this is to make mutually beneficial investments. For example, you could provide a retailer with free product display fixtures. Or you could develop a networked computer system to share sales data in real time with your entire supply chain.

With so much potential for conflicts of interest among channel members, it's crucial to emphasize teamwork, empathy, and trust. This can help all your channel members focus on their common interests, and work together to optimize the productivity of the channel as a whole.

Chapter 11

What Are Your Strategic Priorities?

Can you imagine a business that does not need sales revenue to survive? There aren't many. If your firm is like most, then your sales revenue is the lifeblood of your business.

You probably devote considerable resources to generating sales. And naturally, you want the greatest possible return on the resources you invest. So you need to use your resources efficiently.

But efficiency alone is not enough. If you are working on a hopeless task, no amount of efficiency will bring you success. Therefore, right from the outset, you should be careful to apply your resources and effort to goals that are both achievable and potentially profitable.

To do that, you'll need to accurately assess your firm's capabilities. Next, you'll need to match your capabilities with your most promising opportunities. In other words, you'll need to identify markets that you are capable of serving exceptionally well.

Target With Care

Why should you be so careful when selecting markets to target? Because if you choose a market that is unsuitable, you could waste your effort and resources on an endeavor that lacks promise. In contrast, if you choose well, then your effort could be richly rewarded.

For example, if you choose to launch an unremarkable product in a declining market that is beset by overcapacity and cutthroat price competition, your prospects will be dim, no matter what resources you commit. But if instead you launch a well-positioned product in a large, growing market with no significant competitors, you will likely achieve much better results.

In fact, your choice of which markets or segments to target is one of the most important marketing decision you will need to make. This decision will have a far-reaching impact on every aspect of your marketing effort, and on the long-term profitability of your firm.

Primary Strategic Decisions

Imagine for example that one idle Sunday afternoon, while attempting to bake your own avocado cheesecake from scratch, the ingredients unexpectedly coalesce into a new kind of toothpaste. After containing your initial outburst of hysterical glee, you resolve to rationally evaluate the market potential of your new concoction. You hire a market research firm to assess the competitiveness and profitability of the toothpaste market, and to identify any poorly-served segments that might find your avocado-flavored toothpaste irresistible.

The results, you are pleased to learn, indicate that, though the toothpaste market is dominated by entrenched rivals of gargantuan size, a substantial *segment* of teens and twentysomethings is eager for a new toothpaste adventure. Based on this insight, you make your **primary strategic decisions**: You will *target* young people, aged 15 to 25, with a new tropical-fruit-flavored toothpaste line. And you will *position* your product as a fun way for young people to avoid cavities, while scenting their breath with exotic tropical aromas. The segmentation, targeting, and positioning choices you have made are considered *primary* strategic decisions because of their far-reaching and long-term impact.

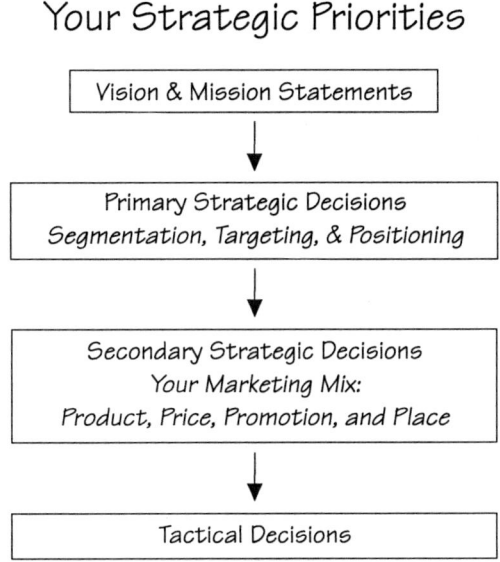

Secondary Strategic Decisions

Having made your primary strategic decisions, you next turn your attention to your marketing mix, including your product, price, promotion, and distribution channels. Your marketing mix decisions are of secondary strategic significance. They must be consistent with the primary strategic decisions you have already made. And of course, your marketing mix decisions should help you satisfy your customers, ward off competitive threats, and maximize your profits.

With regard to your toothpaste line, the particular marketing mix decisions you must now make include whether to add a guava-flavored variety, how to price your line with respect to a rival's turnip-flavored toothpaste line, whether to use a porcupine mascot as a long-term product association, and whether or not to sell your toothpaste line directly to tropical hotels.

Tactical Decisions

Finally, you will need to make any necessary tactical decisions, detailing how your strategies will be implemented on a daily basis. These will include such decisions as whether to put your product on sale this week in Tahiti, whether to advertise in the October issue of the Tennessee Journal of Toothpaste Technology, and whether or not to secure more shelf space in Barney's Foods in Butte, Montana.

Tactical decisions normally have a limited, short-term impact. This is in contrast to the far-reaching, long-term impact of strategic decisions. However, there is no clear dividing line separating strategic and tactical decisions. Some decisions are strategic, some are tactical, and others are a bit of both. What's important is that you should always start with your primary strategic decisions, because they will determine the overall allocation of your marketing resources. And if you allocate your resources to the most promising opportunities, your subsequent secondary strategic decisions and tactical efforts will be more likely to prove effective.

Keep Your Strategies Flexible

In the course of interacting with your customers and rivals, you may sense a need to adjust your tactics occasionally, especially if your business environment is constantly changing. However, be careful that your tactics do not deviate too much, pulling your strategies off course. This can prevent you from reaching your long-term goals.

It's best to keep your strategies flexible and responsive to your changing environment, so that your tactics don't have to lead the way. For example, rather than allowing your prestige brand to get caught up in a tactical price war, a more effective strategic approach might entail introducing a fighting brand, which will be discussed in the next chapter.

Chapter 12

Strategies for Gaining and Retaining Market Share

There are two basic types of marketing opportunities that should interest you:
- Opportunities to win *new* customers, and
- Opportunities to retain your *existing* customers.

In order to win new customers, you will need to employ **offensive strategies**. These are strategies that will help you enter new markets or increase your market share. Offensive strategies normally require considerable effort. After making this effort, you will no doubt want to retain the customers that you have won. Most companies prefer to retain their customers because retaining them is much cheaper than attracting new ones.[12]

Therefore, in tandem with your offensive strategies, you should employ **defensive strategies** as well, to retain the customers that you have worked so hard to acquire.

On the other hand, some firms sell products, such as concert grand pianos, that are typically purchased just once in a lifetime. Repeat business may be relatively unimportant for these companies. But they may nonetheless depend heavily on the recommendations of their previous customers – and their piano tuners – in order to attract new business. This is one good reason why they should treat their customers as well as they would if they wanted their repeat business. If they do treat them well, then their customers will be more likely to recommend the firm to their friends. In effect, these firms get their repeat business in the form of recommendations. Hence, these firms need defensive strategies that retain not so much the customers themselves as their goodwill.

Does Growth Require Investment?

As already noted, the purpose of offensive strategies is to acquire new customers. One approach to attracting new customers is to increase advertising or sales activity. This typically costs money. Another approach is to sacrifice margins by discounting your prices. In either case, you will have to forgo current profits in the hope of achieving larger profits in future years.

Is there any other way? Sometimes, yes. If you have a breakthrough product that attracts mass-media interest, then you may have much less need for paid advertising. For example, both Microsoft and Apple have been notably successful at attracting mass-media news coverage for their new product launches. This tactic has no doubt resulted in free media exposure worth millions of dollars over the years. They have been able to attract this coverage partly because their products have a reputation for being able to excite consumer interest.

Another approach to acquiring new customers at little cost is word-of-mouth advertising. This involves generating such a high level of enthusiasm about your product among your customers that they feel compelled to talk about it to their friends. While most successful companies depend on word-of-mouth advertising to some extent, YouTube and FaceBook have excelled at this approach.

A variant of word-of-mouth advertising can be found on websites like Dell.com. On these websites, customers can post product critiques for anyone to see – instantaneously. As a result, products that receive positive reviews can enjoy substantial sales increases with little promotional effort.

However, in order to achieve significant, sustained growth, most firms must employ offensive strategies that entail some financial sacrifice in the short term to achieve long-term gains.

Strategic Effort

All marketing strategies, whether offensive or defensive, require effort. The kind of effort you make will determine the kind of results you achieve. Here is a list of the most important categories of effort that tend to be emphasized in various offensive and defensive marketing strategies:

Effort	Typical Results
Innovation	Superior products and services.
Efficiency	Low costs, low prices, speed, and accuracy.
Customer Relationship Management	Personalized service, convenience, and emotional satisfaction.
Persuasion and Coordination	Influence on customers, suppliers, intermediaries, rivals, and governments.

These categories are not mutually exclusive. You may be able to employ strategies from all four categories at once, though you would probably emphasize some more than others, depending on your circumstances.

Can You Grow In a Mature Market?

In a growing market, firms will typically try to grow by attracting first-time customers. To grow in a declining market, you can target the customers of rival firms that have exited or gone bankrupt. But in a mature market that is not growing at all, you will be able to grow only by winning market share from your rivals.

However, this will not necessarily entail attracting their existing customers. This is because even a mature market will have some new, first-time customers. They will be entering the market at roughly the same rate as other existing customers lose interest, stop purchasing, and exit. Since these new customers will tend to have no established loyalties, they will be the easiest ones to acquire. If you can acquire them faster than you lose your departing customers, your market share will grow, albeit slowly. In other words, because mature markets typically do not grow, any net gain in your customers will increase your market share.

Choose the Path of Least Resistance

If you want to grow more rapidly, you can attempt to win your rivals' customers. However, there is one particular approach that you should normally avoid: Don't try to match a rival's marketing mix in order to attract their best-served and most loyal customers. Such a frontal attack will likely give you no particular advantage, and prove to be expensive and futile. (That said, you might succeed anyway if your firm is much larger, more capable, and more agile.)

In most cases, you would be better off employing a flanking strategy. This would involve targeting customers that your rivals consider unimportant, or who are being neglected. As they are likely dissatisfied, they will be easier to attract. Assuming that they are potentially profitable customers, you will achieve a much better return on your marketing effort by targeting them.

Examples of poorly-served markets might include people with sensitive digestion who want bland, fat-free restaurant food; environmentally concerned drivers who want solar-powered cars; and pilots who need quiet, electric-powered airplanes for flying over noise-sensitive residential areas.

The Flanking Attack Trap

If a rival directs a flanking attack against one of your weaker products, what should you do? Before responding, consider what you risk losing if the attack succeeds. If you will lose only customers that you consider unimportant, then perhaps you should not respond to the attack at all. On the other hand, if you defend your position vigorously, you might at least be able to dissuade your rivals from launching such attacks in the future.

However, there is a cost: A strong defense may involve expensive product improvement, repositioning, advertising, promotions, and additional sales effort. Substantial resources might need to be redeployed from other higher-priority products, which could weaken their marketing programs and leave them vulnerable. This can lead to strategic disorientation, as you divert your resources and attention away from your priorities. Allowing your strategy to drift in this manner could prevent you from achieving your goals. So if you decide to respond to a flanking attack, you should do so in a measured way that does not involve so much effort that your strategies are thrown off course.

Grow Through Innovation

Another way to grow is through innovation. If you can develop a revolutionary new product, you may be able to leapfrog your rivals' technology, as Apple did when releasing its iPhone®. Alternatively, you might be able to bypass your rivals, as L'Eggs® did by selling their hosiery in distinctively different egg-shaped packaging through more convenient distribution channels – grocery stores instead of department stores.

Such breakthrough innovations can leave the industry pioneers scrambling to catch up. The original early entrants may even experience mixed motives about catching up, if that would entail abandoning their technologies, their production facilities, or their marketing mix.

Can You Combine Innovation and Efficiency?

Innovation depends on creativity, which is rarely an efficient process. Nevertheless, innovation can lead to efficiency, by helping your business grow and operate on a large scale.

Innovation can be compatible with both offensive and defensive strategies. Used offensively, innovative products can open new markets for you. As the pioneer in a new market, you can gain economies of scale and operating experience, and so become more efficient than your rivals.

Used defensively, *incremental* product innovation can help you satisfy and retain your *existing* customers. This is because customers normally prefer products that are kept up to date.

In addition, innovation can help you improve your production *processes*, which can increase your efficiency. Since increased efficiency can reduce your costs, you can price your products more competitively. Low, competitive prices can help you retain your existing customers – and attract new ones as well.

Computer chip makers Intel and AMD pioneered their markets with innovative products. Their innovations led to market leadership. This resulted in superior economies of scale, allowing them to become very efficient. Over the years, they have improved both their products and their production processes with continuous incremental innovations. These innovations have enabled them to protect their respective market leadership positions.

If your firm is not the first mover, and you have developed only a minor innovation, its benefits could be quickly matched by more established rivals with substantial R&D budgets. You may be able to avoid this by focusing on a niche segment that is too small to be of interest to your larger competitors. For instance, to avoid competing with large rivals, an innovative new food product could be adapted for diabetics or people with food allergies. However, the drawback of targeting a niche is that its small size may prevent you from achieving economies of scale.

The impact of your innovations will depend on how radical they are, and on who they appeal to. Here are some points to consider:

- Are your innovations evolutionary or revolutionary? A revolutionary innovation may enable you to establish a highly profitable leadership position in a new market. On the other hand, a single minor innovation – such as a new food product – might enable you to enter a new niche segment.
- Evolutionary or incremental innovations – such as small, steady improvements in a courier's services – tend to be used defensively to retain existing customers. But in the long run, even new customers

can be attracted to the advantages accrued by a long series of evolutionary innovations.
- Quite obviously, an innovation that is of little use to anyone will reap few rewards for your business, no matter how revolutionary it is. Similarly, an innovation that appeals only to an extremely small segment may have limited profit potential.

Defensive Strategies Retain Customers

In contrast to the growth orientation of *offensive* strategies, the purpose of *defensive* strategies is to retain your *existing* customers. The most powerful way to retain your existing customers is to ensure their satisfaction. Their satisfaction will depend on how they feel about your product and its positioning. It will also depend on their experience with your company at every point of contact. The quality of your sales, customer service, and technical support are among the factors that will influence your customers' opinion of your firm.

Even the breadth of your product line may have an impact on customer satisfaction. For example, if your line of jams has just two flavors, your customers might feel that it lacks sufficient variety.

Some firms attempt to retain their customers through loyalty programs, rewarding customers with points or credits for their ongoing business. While a loyalty program is basically a defensive strategy, it can at the same time be offensive, in the sense that it can encourage your existing customers to increase their purchases. Customer loyalty programs are often employed in this way by retail chains and airlines.

Advertising can be both offensive and defensive. This is true when it is used to build brand equity, which can both attract and retain customers. It can also be used offensively, with the principal purpose of attracting new customers, or increasing sales to existing customers. As a defensive strategy, it can be used to remind your customers to repurchase, which can help to maintain a steady level of sales.

Following an entirely different approach, some firms use legal sales contracts as a defensive strategy to retain their customers. This can be appropriate if you are providing a significant benefit at the start of a relationship, and need to recover the cost of this benefit from future profits. For example, new cellphone customers are commonly offered a free phone, provided that they sign a service contract that extends over several years. The contract ensures that the telephone company will earn enough margin from each customer's monthly payments to recover the cost of the free phone.

Defend Yourself with Effective Segmentation

The central purpose of all defensive strategies is to retain customers. This can include warding off competitive threats. To anticipate potential threats, look for weaknesses in your marketing strategies that your rivals might try to exploit. Your rivals may scrutinize your segmentation, your positioning, and every element of your marketing mix. And so you should too.

Keep in mind that your segmentation strategies may need to change over time. At the start of a new product life cycle, it is natural to become focused on educating your customers about your product, on refining your product through successive generations, and on keeping up with demand. Meanwhile, as customers become familiar with your product, their initial fascination or delight can turn into a desire for more features that are better suited to their particular needs. With different customers wanting different features, your market can start to fragment. If this happens, then you will need to review your segmentation strategy.

Chances are, you won't welcome the prospect of re-segmenting your market if it will require an inconvenient change in your plans. But if instead your rivals find a way to re-segment your market, they may win market share at your expense. So be sure to take the initiative.

While reviewing your market segmentation strategy, be sure to review your product positioning as well. If your positioning is not clear, unique, and appealing, it may become the focus of an attack. If a rival can position their product more effectively than yours, they may gain a decisive advantage.

Review Your Marketing Mix

After reviewing your segmentation and positioning strategies, you should review your marketing mix. Among your marketing mix elements, distribution channel issues can be particularly treacherous. If your products are not available in all of the outlets where your customers would like to purchase them, then your customers might purchase your rivals' products instead, even if yours are superior. But if you make your products too widely available, or sell them through incompatible intermediaries, then channel conflict may result. In that case, your rivals may take advantage of the conflict, and attempt to build closer relationships with your dissatisfied intermediaries.

Other marketing mix concerns should include whether your prices are too high or low, and whether your marketing communications are effective. In other words, any weaknesses in your marketing mix could be an opportunity for your rivals. Try to discover these weaknesses before they do.

Do Your Rivals Have Mixed Motives?

Competing with a larger rival may pose daunting challenges. However, your large rivals may have mixed motives that can leave them vulnerable. They may also be set in their ways, overconfident, or too proud to compete with a smaller firm. In addition, if your large rivals are already operating at full capacity, they may be unable to serve their entire market, and you may be free to satisfy the excess demand.

If you introduce a new product with which your rivals can compete only by changing their way of doing business, they may be slow to react. They may be reluctant to adopt new technologies, software, or production equipment, if that would mean abandoning their existing investments. Or they may believe that, in order to compete with you, they would need to introduce a new product that would cannibalize sales of their existing products. If they believe they must hurt their own interests in order to compete with you, then they may experience mixed motives, leaving them indecisive and immobilized.

Encircle Your Rivals

If instead you are the larger firm, and have sufficient resources, one offensive strategy you can try is product encirclement. This entails "surrounding" a rival's product with similar products of your own. For example, if your rival sells pineapple juice, you could launch pineapple pear juice, pineapple persimmon juice, and pineapple papaya juice. Each of these products might attract some of your rival's customers, while at the same time creating enough competition to discourage your rival from expanding their product line.

Of course, rivals may try the same kind of strategy on you. They can encircle you geographically, or by exclusively occupying the most important marketing channels. For example, if you operate a restaurant or a retail store, you could be encircled geographically by a rival who opens outlets nearby yours in every direction. Each of these outlets could attract some of your customers, and together they could significantly reduce your sales.

Or your rivals may attempt distribution channel encirclement, by occupying multiple distribution channels exclusively, to deny you access to your market. For example, imagine that you sell a line of kitchen food containers. You might find that grocery, pharmacy, and hardware retailers devote only limited shelf space to your product category, and so they are willing to carry only one brand. If your rival's products already occupy their store shelves, then you might be prevented from selling through these channels. You might even find that your rival has developed separate brands to closely match each retail chain's positioning. The resulting retailer loyalty could prove a formidable barrier.

How can you defend your firm against an encirclement strategy? Your best defense is to preemptively gain as much ground as possible in advance. You should try to quickly occupy the positions you are interested in, before any rivals have a chance to encircle you. It will be more difficult for your rivals to encircle you if you already occupy a large geographic area, or if you already have an extensive product line, or if you already sell through all the distribution channels that interest you.

Stealth can also work to your advantage, as it may allow you to penetrate your market quietly, without drawing attention to your progress. By the time your rivals notice, it may be too late for them to employ an encirclement strategy. In some markets, one way to avoid being noticed is to forgo mass media and Internet advertising in favor of personal selling and direct mail. These are more discreet, though also typically more expensive.

Secure Exclusive Supplier Access

Another way to confine your rivals is to separate them from their suppliers. For example, if you are a wholesaler, you could negotiate exclusivity on a popular product line so that retailers wanting to carry that line would have no choice but to purchase it from you. Once you have started serving their needs with your exclusive line, you may be able to capture more of each retailer's wholesale business, over time.

You may prefer to focus your effort on serving your customers, rather than on surreptitious competitive maneuvers. Nevertheless, your rivals may not hesitate to use these strategies to confine your own position. Understanding these strategies can help you recognize them and be ready to respond.

Protect Your Prestige Brands

Prestige brands can hold a special magic for your customers. But that magic can be easily lost, if you don't protect your prestige brands' positioning.

Imagine that your firm owns a premium-priced prestige brand. If your market share is being eroded by a rival's low-priced product, how should you respond? You will be less vulnerable if you recognize that anytime you face price competition – especially if your brand is a prestige item – you may feel mixed motives that could leave you immobilized.

Quite possibly, your rival suspects that you do not want to cut your price, for fear of damaging your brand image. And they may also believe that you do not want to sacrifice your margins. Yet if you don't discount your price, they will continue stealing market share from you.

One way out of this predicament is to introduce a **fighting brand** at a lower price to compete with your rival's product. A fighting brand is normally used to protect a high-quality brand that is priced for prestige. Your fighting brand should be sold under an entirely separate brand name, to avoid blurring the positioning of your premium brand. And your fighting brand should be priced competitively against your rival's, to attract and retain the more price-sensitive customers.

A fighting brand can also be used to counter sporadic, short-term **guerrilla tactics**. These can include coupons, discounts, and free samples or gifts. Guerrilla tactics are usually difficult to respond to because they typically run their course quickly. But with a fighting brand permanently in place, you can be well-positioned in advance. Hopefully, your fighting brand will enable you to retain at least some of the price-sensitive customers who would otherwise be enticed by your rival's guerrilla promotions.

The Psychology of Persuasion

Some strategies can wield a psychological impact on your rivals' decision-making. The advantage of this is that changing your rivals' minds will surely prove much easier than fighting their actions. Of course, you should not risk breaking the law by colluding with your rivals to obtain their cooperation. Instead, by demonstrating your intentions and competitive strength in the market, you may be able to convince your rivals to act of their own accord in a manner that is favorable to your interests.

To avoid excessive competition in your market, you can try to dissuade potential rivals from entering in the first place. One way to accomplish this is to pre-announce the construction of new factories, restaurants, or retail outlets, and thereby discourage competitors from making similar investments that would result in overcapacity. If your facilities cannot be easily converted to other uses, then your rivals will believe you are strongly committed to your market, and would have difficulty exiting, even if you wanted to. By raising exit barriers in this way, your rivals should get the impression that your determination will be dogged, if not desperate.

Additional tactics can be helpful in this regard. You can pre-announce a new product, well in advance of its launch date, so that customers will postpone purchases in that category, and so that rivals will consider your segment less attractive. The Xbox®, the iPhone®, and the Windows 95® operating system may all have benefited from pre-launch announcements of this sort.

However, if your firm is small, you will not be able to rely on your size to intimidate your rivals. Consequently, any pre-announcement of your intentions may only give your rivals valuable clues about how to defeat your plans. Thus, if you are small, you may have a greater need for surprise. If you can enter a market without warning, then you may be able to gain some market share and build customer loyalty before your rivals notice and have a chance to react.

On the other hand, smaller firms can sometimes gain an advantage by attracting public sympathy as the underdog in a struggle against a corporate giant. For example, by emphasizing the weakness of their position, Netscape was able to elicit considerable public sympathy in the browser war battle of the late 1990s that they fought against Microsoft. This kind of public sympathy can influence not only consumer purchases, but government legislation as well.

While crucial advantages can be gained by influencing your rivals, it is at least as important to influence your existing and potential customers. To accomplish that, you will need a product that promises and delivers superior customer satisfaction. And every element of your marketing mix will need to support your positioning.

Besides positioning your product, you should also position your firm itself. Customers may prefer a company that is positioned as an innovation leader like Apple, a price leader like Wal-Mart, or a customer relationship leader like Virgin Airlines. Customers tend to prefer firms and products that stand for some meaningful benefit. That is, they prefer clear positioning.

In some circumstances, you may need to influence your lawmakers as well. Industries that depend on patents or copyrights need unambiguous laws to protect their intellectual property. Other industries can be vulnerable to unfair foreign competition. If your firm faces this kind of challenge, you may be able to attain a more favorable business environment by influencing your lawmakers either directly, or through trade associations, in whatever ways are legally permitted.

. . . .

Strategic marketing involves making optimal use of your firm's resources to achieve superior profitability and customer satisfaction in a competitive business environment. However, a truly successful firm will not only create value for itself and its customers, but will do so while protecting our natural environment, observing whatever laws apply, and fostering mutual consideration and respect among all people. With that in mind, you can now start applying what you have learned in this book. Here's to your strategic marketing success!

Notes

1. Yannopoulos, Peter. *Marketing Strategy*. (Thomson Nelson, 2007) p.8. Yannopoulos' work inspired much of the strategic marketing theory presented in this book.

2. Keller, Kevin Lane. *Strategic Brand Management*. (Prentice Hall, 2002 p.120. Keller's work inspired much of the branding theory presented in this book.

3. Kotler, Philip, and Peggy H. Cunningham. *Marketing Management*, Canadian Eleventh Edition. (Prentice Hall, 2003) p.6.

4. Keller, Kevin Lane. *Strategic Brand Management*. (Prentice Hall, 2002.

5. Adapted from Yannopoulos, p.105.

6. Ferrell, O. C. and Michael Hartline. *Marketing Strategy*. (Thomson, 2004) p.140.

7. Keller, p.367.

8. Yannopoulos, p.78.

9. Ries, Al, and Jack Trout. *The 22 Immutable Laws of Marketing*. (HarperBusiness, 1994) p.90.

10. Keller, Kevin Lane. *Strategic Brand Management*. (Prentice Hall, 2002 p.577.

11. Yannopoulos, p.170.

12. Best, Roger J. *Market-Based Management*. (Prentice Hall, 2004) p.15.

Bibliography

Best, Roger J. *Market-Based Management*. (Prentice Hall, 2004)

Coughlan, Anne, Erin Anderson, Louis W. Stern, and Adel El-Ansary. *Marketing Channels*. (Prentice Hall, 2001)

Ferrell, O. C. and Michael Hartline. *Marketing Strategy*. (Thomson, 2004)

Hamel, Gary. *Leading The Revolution*, Revised Edition. (Plume, 2002)

Jain, Subhash C. *Marketing Planning and Strategy*. (Thomson 1999)

Keller, Kevin Lane. *Strategic Brand Management*. (Prentice Hall, 2002)

Kotler, Philip, and Peggy H. Cunningham. *Marketing Management*, Canadian Eleventh Edition. (Prentice Hall, 2003)

Kumar, Nirmalya. *Marketing as Strategy*. (HBS Press, 2004)

McGrath, Rita Gunther, and Ian C MacMillan. *Market Busters*. (HBS Press, 2005)

Moser, Ted, Kevin Mundt, James Quella, and Adrian J. Slywotzky. *Profit Patterns: 30 Ways to Anticipate and Profit from Strategic Forces Reshaping Your Business*. (Crown Business, 1999)

Nohria, Nitin, William F. Joyce, and Bruce Roberson. *What Really Works: The 4+2 Formula for Sustained Business Success*. (HarperCollins, 2003)

Ries, Al, and Jack Trout. The 22 Immutable Laws of Marketing. (HarperBusiness, 1994)

Sommers, Montrose S., and James G. Barnes. *Marketing*. (McGraw-Hill Ryerson, 2003)

Walker, Orville, Jr., Harper Boyd, John Mullins, and Jean-Claude Larreche. *Marketing Strategy: A Decision-Focused Approach*. (McFraw-Hill Irwin, 2002)

Yannopoulos, Peter. *Marketing Strategy*. (Thomson Nelson, 2007)

Index

agents 182
antitrust laws 2
BAM stores 184
brand 21, 81
branded ingredients 67
brand equity 86
brand evangelists 161
brand extension 111
brand rationalization 115
bricks-and-clicks retailer 200
bricks and mortar stores 184
brokers 182
cannibalize 114
category extension 112
CGS 144
chain ratio method 57
channel conflict 189
channel design 195
channel structure 182
cognitive dissonance 76
commoditization 132
consideration set 99
consolidation 130
contribution margin 4
contribution margin per unit 144
core attributes 100
cost of goods sold 144
differentiation 14
direct distribution 182
distribution channels 25, 182
distribution intensity 25
distributors 182
dual distribution 197
early adopters 160

early majority 160
economies of scale 9
exclusive distribution 191
experience curve effects 9
experiential brands 82
fast-moving consumer goods 190
fighting brand 228
fixed capacity 175
flanking attack 13
forward buying 8
four Ps 13
free-riding 189
frontal attack 13
functional benefits 19
functional brands 81
G&A expenses 146
general and administrative costs 146
guerrilla tactics 228
image brands 81
innovators 160
intensive distribution 190
intermediaries 60, 181
laggards 160
late majority 160
life cycle cost 139
lifetime value 143
line extension 111
marketing 31
marketing expenses 145
marketing mix 13, 17
marketing myopia 47
market segment 17
market size 31

mass customization strategy 61
mass-marketing strategy 61
mixed motives 10
multi-channel distribution 198
net contribution 145
network effects 171
niche segment 64
objections 72
offensive strategies 215
opinion leaders 161
opportunity table 48
opportunity triangle 47
organic ranking 205
paid placement 205
pay-per-click advertising 206
penetration pricing 161
perceptual map 88
PLC 3
points of difference 97
points of parity 96
positioning 14
positioning statement 104
price sensitivity 147
primary demand 130
primary strategic decisions 210
product 31
product life cycle 2
psychographics 56
pure-clicks retailer 200
search engine 204
search engine optimization 204
search results 205
secondary demand 130
selective demand 130
selective distribution 191
SEO 204
sequenced entry strategy 61
served market 45
shakeout 12
skim pricing 160
slotting allowance 24
strategic market definition 47
strategic network 170
supplementary imagery 101
switching costs 63
top-of-the-mind awareness 6
total contribution margin 4, 145
variable costs 4
wholesalers 182
word-of-mouth advertising 161